Basic Maintenance and Repair

Basic
Maintenance
and Repair

Simple Techniques
to Make Your Bike Ride Better
and Last Longer

EDITED BY ED PAVELKA

Rodale Press, Inc.
Emmaus, Pennsylvania

© 1999 by Rodale Press, Inc.

Photographs © by Donna Chiarelli, Mel Lindstrom, Paul Schraub

Photograph on pages 126–27 courtesy of Trek Bicycle Corporation

Illustration courtesy of Cane Creek Cycling Components

Cover and Interior Designer: Susan P. Eugster

Cover Photographer: Kurt Wilson/Rodale Images

Interior Photographers: Donna Chiarelli, Mel Lindstrom, Mitch Mandel/Rodale Images, Paul Schraub

Cover photograph taken at Bike Line, Allentown, Pennsylvania

Library of Congress Cataloging-in-Publication Data

    Bicycling magazine's basic maintenance and repair : simple techniques to make your bike ride better and last longer / edited by Ed Pavelka.
       p.   cm.
    Includes index.
    ISBN 1–57954–170–4 paperback
    1. Bicycles—Maintenance and repair.   I. Pavelka, Ed.   II. Bicycling.
TL430.B54   1999
629.28'772—dc21   99–35338

Distributed to the book trade by St. Martin's Press

2   4   6   8   10 9 7 5 3 1   paperback

Visit us on the Web at www.rodalesportsandfitness.com, or call us toll-free at (800) 848-4735.

OUR PURPOSE

We inspire and enable people to improve their lives and the world around them.

Contents

PART FIVE

Internal Bearings

PART SIX

Mountain Bike Particulars

PART SEVEN

Detailing

PART EIGHT

Special Service

Introduction

Much has changed in cycling equipment since Rodale published the first version of this book in 1990. One result is that bikes are more reliable than ever. Thanks to the technological innovations sparked by mountain bikes, many components work better for longer periods of time because they're designed to withstand the onslaught of dirt and moisture. A prime example is the proliferation of sealed bearings in cranksets, headsets, hubs, and pedals as well as improved seals in conventional loose-ball designs.

All of this doesn't mean that a bike no longer needs routine maintenance and an occasional repair. Far from it. But some of the procedures are different. This book brings you up to date. If your bike is relatively new, you'll find directions appropriate for your modern components. If you have an older bike that you want to keep running well, don't worry—this updated version hasn't omitted anything that you need to know.

To use this book, you'll need some general and specialized tools. That's what chapter 1 is all about. Once your home shop is equipped, start each repair by reading the procedure all the way through, then go step-by-step as you work. In most cases, each chapter contains a list of tools and supplies so you can double-check that you have everything that's necessary. These lists are comprehensive. You may not need every item listed for a given procedure in order to service your bike's particular components.

As you work, you'll find that bike maintenance improves your confidence. You'll understand how your bike functions and know that the chances of something going wrong on a ride are greatly reduced. If there should be a problem, you'll know you can handle it. Routine service also avoids the wasteful expense caused by neglect, helping your bike last longer as well as work better. These are terrific payoffs for becoming a home mechanic.

PART ONE

Routine Service

1
Designing a Home Shop

Three California couples enjoy bicycle repair so much that they team up to rent a 500-square-foot storage space for $110 a month to use as a workshop. It has plenty of room for their tandem, mountain, and road bikes—all 17 of them.

Every winter, they strip the bikes to their frames and rebuild them. On some weekends, you can find all six of these equipment enthusiasts spending hours cleaning parts, patching tires, and simply having a good time. Sometimes they fix friends' bikes, but always for the pleasure of tinkering, not to make money.

While you may not take to bicycle maintenance with such passion, a properly equipped, well-organized shop will at least make it enjoyable. A home work area will also save you money, and the technical knowledge you gain will add a deeper dimension to your cycling.

Do You Need a Shop?

The more bikes in your household and the more they're used, the greater the benefits of a home shop. Most bike shops base labor rates at $40 to $65 per hour, so it won't take many do-it-yourself repairs to defray the cost of setting up your own shop. This chapter details complete home shop setups costing $500 or more, but you can proceed piecemeal, buying only those bike-specific tools that you need often and know how to use. If you already have common items such as screwdrivers, pliers, and wrenches, the cash outlay will be reduced considerably.

Of course, having the tools doesn't guarantee that you'll perform flawless work. But your chances are good because basic repairs require only average mechanical skills. This book provides plenty of information to handle most jobs like a pro. If you really get into it and want in-depth detail with full illustrations, check out the latest edition of *Bicycling Magazine's Complete Guide to Bicycle Maintenance and Repair* by Jim Langley.

A shop can be set up anywhere at home. If you don't have the space or money to create a shop, call local bike stores to see if they provide customer repair areas. Sometimes there's a fee but you'll

probably still save money. What's more, if something goes wrong, replacement parts and helpful shop personnel are close by. Check with
your local bike club, too. Some have repair facilities for use by mem-
bers, sort of a community version of the space rented by the three
California couples.

Working Environment

Select an area large enough to provide walking space around the bike,
plus room for a workbench and shelves or a table. (Your bench will be
constantly cluttered if it's the only place available on which to put
things.) Screw rubber-coated storage hooks (ask for "bike hooks" at
shops) into the rafters to hang extra wheels and bikes so they're out of
the way.

Shag carpet or wood floors with cracks can swallow small parts. A
light-colored, stain-resistant surface is best. Indoor/outdoor carpet is
another good choice. It supplies some cushion and can be washed or replaced when soiled. Hang an inexpensive fluorescent fixture over the
workbench to ensure good lighting.

Building supply stores sell workbench kits, or you can make your
own bench for a few dollars less. A good size is 8- by 2-foot and about
38 inches high. (A smaller surface will work if space is tight, but it will
get cluttered faster.) Use 4- by 4-inch legs and 2- by 4-inch cross braces.
Build a storage shelf on the bottom for your toolbox, trash bin, and
spare parts.

Mount a tool board on the wall over the workbench. A 4- by 8-foot
sheet of ¾-inch plywood works better than pegboard, which requires
mounting hardware that can limit your tool arrangement. Use a large
piece of cardboard as a template. Place it on the floor and arrange your
tools on it, placing the most frequently used ones in the center. Then
draw outlines around the tools. Tack the template to the board, then
drive finishing nails into the outlines in positions that will support the
tools. Remove the template, hang the tools, and trace their outlines on
the board with a black marker. Then you'll know exactly where each
tool goes, keeping your work area neat and efficient. Finish by making a
holder for your screwdrivers and allen wrenches. All this takes is a short
length of 2-by-4. Drill small-diameter holes in the 2-by-4 for the tools
to drop into, then attach it to the big board.

Repair Stands

A pro mechanic wouldn't think of working without a good repair stand that elevates the bike and allows both wheels to spin. Better stands also let you rotate the bike to any position. Various models are made by Wrench Force, Park, Minoura, and other companies. Stands costing less than $75 are usually less stable and adjustable. Most stands fold for travel and storage. More expensive stands are usually durable, fit uncommon tubing diameters, allow different methods of grasping the bike, and provide enough stability to tug and pound.

Think through your needs and spend enough to get a stand that meets all of them. Remember, you'll be working with your stand for years.

If your space is tight, consider a bike clamp that mounts to the bench or wall. These are usually less expensive than full stands. They may let you rotate the bike, but you'll have to take the bike down and turn it around to work on the opposite side.

Tools

Basic repairs require household tools plus a few specialty items that are available at bike shops. Save money on any hand tools you need by picking up used ones at flea markets, swap meets, or yard sales. Otherwise, buy tools at a store that's having a sale. Basic cycling tools are stocked by most shops (some items may need to be ordered) and by mail-order companies such as Bike Nashbar in Youngstown, Ohio; Colorado Cyclist in Colorado Springs; Performance Bicycle in Chapel Hill, North Carolina; or Excel Sports in Boulder, Colorado. For the largest selection, get a catalog from the Third Hand in Ashland, Oregon. This company also sells many hard-to-find small parts, plus repair manuals and instructional videos.

The tool lists have been broken down into lists for basic, intermediate, and ultimate home shops. The basic set will let you do most routine repairs. The intermediate group will enable you to change cogs and do other less common tasks. The ultimate group is sufficient for any job. You'll also need grease, oil, cutting oil (if you plan to tap or chase threads), acetone, a sponge, a flashlight, rubber bands, small stick-on labels, detergent, a bucket, a toothbrush, a felt-tip pen, indelible marker, and chrome polish.

When possible, use rags to wipe parts clean, rather than resorting to solvents. If you do need the latter, use biodegradable degreasers (available at hardware stores, bike shops, or the above mail-order companies). Kerosene is inexpensive and readily available but requires rubber gloves

Tools and Supplies for the Home Shop

BASIC
General Tools
- [ ] Phillips screwdrivers (small, medium)
- [ ] flathead screwdrivers (small, medium, large)
- [ ] regular pliers
- [ ] Channellock pliers
- [ ] needle-nose pliers
- [ ] Vise-Grip pliers
- [ ] diagonal cutters
- [ ] allen wrenches (2.5-, 3-, 4-, 5-, 6-, 7-, and 8-mm)
- [ ] combination wrenches (7- through 17-mm)
- [ ] adjustable wrenches (6- and 12-inches)
- [ ] ball-peen hammer (8-ounce)
- [ ] plastic mallet
- [ ] scissors
- [ ] tape measure (in centimeters and inches)
- [ ] hacksaw
- [ ] files (small, flat; and medium, coarse)
- [ ] punches
- [ ] awl
- [ ] chain lube
- [ ] WD-40
- [ ] emery cloth
- [ ] fine steel wool
- [ ] sandpaper

- [ ] electrical tape
- [ ] 12-inch ruler
- [ ] socket wrench set
- [ ] oil can or turkey baster
- [ ] rubbing alcohol
- [ ] utility knife
- [ ] assortment of small paintbrushes
- [ ] small wire brush
- [ ] rustproof primer
- [ ] goggles
- [ ] rubber gloves
- [ ] biodegradable solvent
- [ ] ⅜-inch-drive ratchet
- [ ] Teflon lube

Bicycle Tools
- [ ] this book
- [ ] repair stand
- [ ] tire pump with gauge
- [ ] tire levers
- [ ] pedal wrench
- [ ] cone wrenches (two pairs, usually 13- and 18-mm for front and rear hubs, respectively)
- [ ] Schrader valve core remover
- [ ] cable cutters
- [ ] third-hand tool or toe strap (for brake cable adjustments)
- [ ] chain rivet extractor
- [ ] cassette remover (for your brand)
- [ ] two chain whips (for changing cogs)

and adequate ventilation. All solvents should be kept in clearly marked containers and disposed of in an environmentally sound way. (Check the front of the phone book or your neighborhood gas station for more information.)

- ☐ spoke wrench
- ☐ crankarm bolt wrench
  (for bikes with crankarm bolts)
- ☐ crankarm removal tool
- ☐ bottom bracket adjustment tools
  (lockring and fixed cup spanners,
  plus pin tool or cartridge lockring
  tool for sealed units)
- ☐ headset wrench (usually 32-mm)
- ☐ linseed oil or spoke thread
  lubricant/adhesive
- ☐ shock pump
- ☐ handlebar tape
- ☐ touch-up paint
- ☐ rubbing compound
- ☐ frame wax
- ☐ Weigle Frame Saver
- ☐ spray polish
- ☐ Simichrome
- ☐ tire mounting glue

INTERMEDIATE
Includes all "Basic" tools, plus:

- ☐ *Bicycling Magazine's Complete
  Guide to Bicycle Maintenance
  and Repair*
- ☐ wheel truing stand
- ☐ Stein fixed cup wrench clamp
- ☐ small needle-type grease gun
  (for lubricating parts with grease
  holes or fittings)
- ☐ bench vise

ULTIMATE
Includes all "Basic" and
"Intermediate" tools, plus:

- ☐ *Sutherland's Handbook
  for Bicycle Mechanics*
- ☐ dishing gauge
  (for building wheels)
- ☐ spoke tensiometer
  (for building wheels)
- ☐ dropout alignment tool
- ☐ headset installation and
  removal tools
- ☐ derailleur-hanger alignment tool
- ☐ rear-triangle alignment
  indicator bar
- ☐ electric drill and bits
- ☐ grinder with wire and buffing
  wheels
- ☐ air compressor with blower
  attachment
- ☐ metric ruler
- ☐ solvent tank
- ☐ vernier caliper
- ☐ metric taps (5-mm by 0.8-mpt
  and 6-mm by 1.0-mpt)
- ☐ freewheel remover
- ☐ freewheel vise
- ☐ pedal axle tool
- ☐ No. 10 Torx driver
  (for Time and Look pedals)
- ☐ snap-on chain cleaner
- ☐ cartridge retainer ring tool

2
Weekly Maintenance

During much of the year, you probably ride several times each week. To keep your bike working efficiently and reliably, devote a few minutes each week to cleaning, lubricating, and adjusting it. This general maintenance will also help you find a problem before it results in a breakdown. If a repair is necessary, consult the appropriate chapter for instructions.

Clean the Machine

Put your bike in a repair stand or against a support. Unless the frame is filthy, simply wipe it down with a soft rag. To cut through tough stuff like dried sweat or sports drink, spritz the rag with spray-on furniture polish or use a cleaner wax made for bikes. (Unlike car waxes, bike waxes don't leave chalky residue in hard-to-wipe places.) If the bike is dirty because it's been ridden in rain or mud, wash it with a soft brush and mild detergent, then rinse and dry.

Work down from the top of the bike, saving the drivetrain (crankset, chain, and derailleurs) for last because these parts are usually the dirtiest. When the frame is clean, inspect for frame damage. Look for bulges in the metal or telltale cracks in the paint, especially at tube intersections. If you find any, have the problem evaluated by a pro mechanic. To prevent rust on a steel frame or simply preserve a nice appearance, use touch-up paint on scratches or chips that expose bare metal.

Next, put on your goggles and gloves and dip a corner of a rag in biodegradable solvent or spray it with a thin lubricant such as WD-40. Wipe each metal component clean, inspecting for cracks, loose bolts, or other problems.

Do not clean rims with solvent, which can leave a slippery film that renders the brakes useless. Instead, wipe the rims with a clean, dry rag. Or, if they're oily, clean them with alcohol, which cuts oil and grease and evaporates. Inspect each spoke hole for cracks and for ferrules that may be pulling through (if your rims have these fittings). Look for dents, gouges, and cracks in the sidewalls. Replace a damaged rim immediately because it could fail during a ride—with painful consequences.

Check Components

Once the cleaning is finished, check out the major parts of the bike.

Brakes. Firmly squeeze each brake lever, trying to pull it to the handlebar. Anything pop loose? Check that each pad makes flush contact with the rim and recedes about 4 mm when the lever is released. You don't need tools to make minor brake adjustments. Just turn the barrels on the calipers or brake levers.

Wheels. Wiggle each spoke and squeeze pairs to find any that are broken or loose. Spin each wheel and watch the rim where it passes through the brake pads. If you see large wobbles or hops, true the wheel before riding again, or the rim could become bent beyond repair. Check for loose hub bearings by wiggling the wheel from side to side. There should be no more than a hint of play.

Tires. Inflate to full pressure as labeled on the sidewall. Examine each tire's tread for embedded glass or other debris. Potential puncture producers can often be flicked out before they work through the casing to the tube. Also check the tread and sidewalls for cuts, bulges, and excessive wear. Damaged tires must be replaced immediately. Their failure is inevitable (and you can count on the blowout happening at the worst possible time). If you have tubular tires (road tires that are glued onto the rim), try to push them off the rim with your thumbs. If they budge, reglue them.

Headset. Check the headset adjustment by squeezing the front-brake lever hard while rocking the bike back and forth. Clunking means looseness. If it sounds okay, grasp the top tube, lift the front of the bike a couple of inches, and nudge the handlebar to the right and then to the left. It should pivot fully in each direction and not catch when it passes through the straight-ahead position. A headset that's tight or notchy reduces steering control, so fix it right away. Place an ear against the tip of the saddle and turn the handlebar. Rumbling means the headset bearings are dry or dirty.

Crankset. Grasp a crankarm and wiggle it from side to side. There shouldn't be play. A loose crankset will impair shifting and wear out prematurely. Check the tightness of each crankarm's fixing bolt as well as the little bolts that attach the chainrings. Once a month, remove the pedals, set the chain down around the frame, and check the condition of the bottom bracket bearings by putting your ear to the saddle as you turn the crankset. If there's a loud roar or clattering, the bearings need service.

Pedals. While the pedals are off, turn their axles and feel for roughness or looseness. Inspect the cleat-retention mechanisms for wear as you wipe out trapped dirt. Put a drop of chain lube on each hinge, then wipe off any excess. If your bike has toeclips instead of clipless pedals, check them for cracks and loose bolts. Check the straps for wear and damaged buckles. Grease pedal threads before re-installation.

Accessories. Grasp the saddle by the tip and tail. Shake it in all directions. Do the same with the handlebar. Tighten anything that slips. Check the nuts and bolts on accessories such as bottle cages, racks, and your computer. Make sure there's a fresh tube and patch kit in your seatbag.

Lube and Inflate

The two surest (and simplest) ways to help your bike work well are to maintain proper tire pressure and periodically lubricate your chain. A lubed chain shifts better, runs quieter, and lasts longer. Full tires roll efficiently and protect your rims from damage when riding over hard objects.

Chain care. This is a simple matter of wiping the links clean with a rag, then applying the lubricant of your choice. It can be done with the chain on the bike. If the chain is filled with sludge, however, you'll need

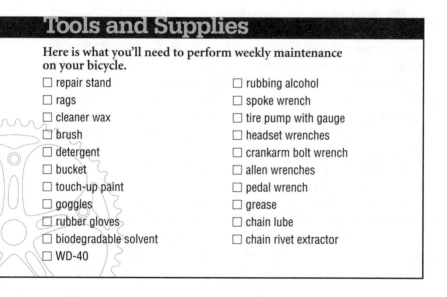

Tools and Supplies

Here is what you'll need to perform weekly maintenance on your bicycle.

- ☐ repair stand
- ☐ rags
- ☐ cleaner wax
- ☐ brush
- ☐ detergent
- ☐ bucket
- ☐ touch-up paint
- ☐ goggles
- ☐ rubber gloves
- ☐ biodegradable solvent
- ☐ WD-40

- ☐ rubbing alcohol
- ☐ spoke wrench
- ☐ tire pump with gauge
- ☐ headset wrenches
- ☐ crankarm bolt wrench
- ☐ allen wrenches
- ☐ pedal wrench
- ☐ grease
- ☐ chain lube
- ☐ chain rivet extractor

to remove it and use a solvent. Wipe down the chainring teeth and rear derailleur pulleys while the chain is off. Waxy lubes that go on wet but become dry to the touch streamline chain maintenance by preventing a gunky buildup, but they aren't the best choice if you ride in a damp climate. An oily lube protects better in the wet.

Air pressure. Recommended tire inflation is usually 100 to 110 pounds per square inch (psi) for road bike tires, while mountain bike tires take about half that much. Check information on the tire sidewall. Most tire pumps with built-in gauges are reasonably accurate. The pumps at gas stations are risky to use because they quickly deliver a large volume of air, which can blow out a bike tire.

Once you've established your weekly maintenance routine, the work will take only about 20 minutes. This small amount of time pays off big in confidence, safety, and smooth, efficient riding.

3
Quick Drivetrain Cleaning and Lubing

A bike's drivetrain includes the rear hub with cassette or freewheel, crankset, chain, derailleurs, and pedals. Assuming you don't crash and damage it, this system will run smoothly for thousands of miles if you clean and lube it regularly. You could just add more oil when the chain looks dry, as many cyclists do. But by getting rid of the built-up gunk first, you rid the parts of the main cause of premature wear.

Here's an easy clean-and-lube procedure that will ensure that you get more performance and life from your drivetrain. As a bonus, you won't get nearly as grimy when removing the rear wheel to fix a flat. Do this maintenance about once a month when you're riding regularly, or whenever you notice a sludgy buildup of grime on the chain and derailleur pulleys. (*Note:* This procedure won't revive a worn-out drivetrain. If you have several thousand miles on your bike, you should at least install a new chain and, if necessary, any cogs that are too worn to mesh with it. Then start this regular maintenance.)

Measure the chain. Put the bike in your repair stand and shift into the smallest chainring/cog combination. If you're unsure of your chain's condition, measure it. Put a ruler's first mark on the center of any pin, then look at the 12-inch mark (see photo). It should also be on the center of a pin. Friction wears down the working parts, making them smaller, which allows a chain to stretch. If the center of the latter pin is ⅛ inch or more past the 12-inch mark, replace the chain.

Clean the chain. Working on the section of chain below the chainstay, scrub about four links at a time. First, hold a rag behind the chain and spray the links with WD-40 to help dissolve the grime. If necessary, use a toothbrush to dislodge any stubborn stuff. (Always save your old toothbrushes for your toolbox.) Wipe the links clean with the rag, then move to the next section. Continue until you've cleaned the whole chain.

Clean the chainring. Lift the chain off the chainring and rest it on the bottom bracket, which will let you get at both rings with a rag. Use the toothbrush and a small screwdriver to dislodge gunk. Use WD-40 to dissolve tough deposits. Slide a rag between and through the rings to reach difficult spots. Wipe the rings, spider, and crankarms clean. Put the chain back on the small ring.

Clean the pedals. Spray WD-40 on the surface of clipless pedals and wipe them clean with a rag. Dig out any embedded dirt with the screwdriver. Apply a drop of chain lube to the hinges of the cleat-retention mechanisms. For toeclips and straps, put a drop on the buckle.

Clean the front derailleur. Slide a rag through the front derailleur's cage and wipe away grime with a back-and-forth action. Remove gunk from the arms with WD-40 and the toothbrush. Lightly lube the derailleur's pivots. Finish by wiping any mess from the bottom bracket.

Clean the cogs. To work on the cogs, you first must remove the rear wheel. Open the brake quick-release, open the hub quick-release, and push the wheel out while holding the rear derailleur back. Place the wheel on your lap or workbench with the cogs up. Lightly spritz the cogs with WD-40 to loosen gunk. After a minute, brush the teeth, then slide a rag back and forth in a shoe-shine motion between each pair of cogs. This will cause the cogs to rotate so everything gets cleaned. Also wipe the face of the smallest cog, the back of the largest, and the hub. Reinstall the wheel.

Clean the rear derailleur. Spray the pulleys with WD-40, then hold a rag on the exposed edge of each one as you pedal backward by hand, causing the pulleys to spin and release their gunk. Continue to spray and wipe as necessary. Then work the rag around and through the derailleur cage and body to clean it thoroughly. Lightly lube the pivot points and pulley hubs.

Lube the chain. Complete the job by hand-pedaling backward and putting one drop of chain lube on top of each pin as the chain passes under the chainstay. When finished, gently spin the chain for a few seconds to help the lube work in, then hold a clean rag around it to wipe off the excess. If possible, wait a few hours and wipe the chain again before riding. This will reduce the amount of lube that slings onto the frame and rear wheel as well as the amount of new dirt the chain picks up.

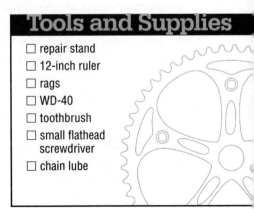

Tools and Supplies

- ☐ repair stand
- ☐ 12-inch ruler
- ☐ rags
- ☐ WD-40
- ☐ toothbrush
- ☐ small flathead screwdriver
- ☐ chain lube

4

Silencing Mysterious Noises

There's nothing more annoying than the cryptic sounds that can haunt even a well-maintained bicycle. For example, one of the *Bicycling* magazine editors was bothered by a rhythmic click that seemed to be coming from the crankset of his megabucks titanium bike. He heard it each time he stood while climbing. After rebuilding the bottom bracket not once but twice, to no avail, he remembered that on rare occasions such noises can come from a clamp-on–type front derailleur—like the one on his bike. He loosened the fixing bolt just enough to let a drop of lube seep between the clamp and frame. Voilà—his bike has been quiet ever since. He could have averted two fruitless crankset overhauls if he'd thought of this 1-minute procedure first (or even second), but that's what makes noise elimination an interesting game.

Drivetrain cleanliness and lubrication will keep the usual suspects running smoothly and quietly, but what about those other frustrating ticks, clicks, creaks, chirps, squeals, buzzes, and rattles that occasionally occur? Here's a slew of tricks to try.

Drivetrain and Pedal Ticks

This ticking is a metallic click or snap during every crankarm revolution. You may even be able to feel it through your foot. Remember, a click isn't from the chain if it occurs at the same place on each pedal stroke. You should check the following things.

Loose connections. Unscrew each pedal, grease the threads, and retighten it firmly to the crankarm. (Don't forget that the left pedal has backward threads. Turn it clockwise to unscrew, counterclockwise to install.) Next, tighten the crankarm bolt, the big bolt that holds the crankarm onto the bottom bracket axle. To get at it, you may have to remove a dustcap with an allen wrench or screwdriver. Finally, check the tightness of the small bolts that connect the chainrings. Even better, remove each one, grease it, and reinstall it.

Bottom bracket. If the crankarms have lateral play even though they are tight on the bottom bracket axle, the bearings are not properly adjusted. You may hear this excessive movement during pedaling. Correct the problem using the information in chapter 18 or 19, depending on your equipment.

Bad ball bearings. Bearings, either loose or in cartridges, are found in the pedals and bottom bracket. Their lubrication can get contaminated or dry up, and they can become scored or oval with wear. For these reasons, always install new bearings every time you overhaul a part. Also, check the bearing races that loose balls roll in. If you see uneven wear, replace the races as well as the bearings.

Front derailleur. Spray it with a penetrating lubricant and get some between the clamp and seat tube. Tighten firmly. As our editor learned, a dry or loose front derailleur can make a ticking sound during hard pedaling.

Rear derailleur. The pulleys spin many times during each minute of riding. They can squeak (and increase drivetrain friction) if they dry out. Drip or spray lube into the edge of the cap on each side of both pulleys (see photo). *Note:* This isn't necessary if you see the word "sealed" on the pulleys.

Pedals. If greasing the pedal threads and tightening them firmly doesn't help, lube the hinges of the clipless type or the joints between

the frame and body of the conventional variety. Do the same where toe-clips attach, after making sure the bolts are tight.

Cleats. Squeaks or creaks that occur during pedaling can be caused by the interface of clipless pedals and cleats. Often, this is a signal of worn cleats, and replacing them will stop the noise. You can also try cleaning the contact area of each pedal and lubing the hinges. Make sure the bolts that hold the cleats to the shoes are tight. Rubbing paraffin on the cleats can silence creaky friction against the pedals, but it causes grit to stick when you walk, which ultimately increases wear. It's better to wax the pedal surface or spray on silicone and wipe off the excess.

Chain Clicks

A chain that chirps like a scene from *The Birds* is simply in need of lubrication. This should never happen if you're servicing your bike regularly, but it might occur if lube gets washed off during a ride in the rain. Always wipe down and relube the chain after a wet ride.

A consistent click or skip in the drivetrain that doesn't occur in sequence with your pedal stroke usually means a stiff chain link. Again, this should be a very rare problem if you're servicing the chain correctly. Here's a three-step procedure to find and fix this problem.

1. Kneel on the right side of the bike and turn the crankarm backward. Carefully watch where the chain wraps around the cog and winds through the derailleur pulleys. A frozen, unbending link will be apparent.

2. Stop when the stiff link is midway between the derailleur and chainring. Grasp the chain on either side of the link (use rags to keep your hands cleaner) and flex it to-and-fro laterally until it moves as freely as the other links.

3. Douse the formerly tight link with your chain lube, then make sure to keep the entire chain properly maintained using the guidelines in chapters 3 and 13. Tight links are more likely to occur if the chain is improperly installed or allowed to become dry or rusty.

Handlebar Hubbub

Handlebar snapping or creaking usually occurs when you're sprinting or climbing, either pulling hard on the handlebar or putting more weight on it. Here's what you need to check.

Handlebar/stem junction. Make sure the stem's binder bolt is tight. If the noise persists, undo the bolt, grease its threads, put grease between the bar and stem, and tighten firmly. Some bars have a separate center ferrule (the section where the stem clamps). This can loosen and creak. You might be able to silence it by spraying lube along the edges of the ferrule, but you should still have a professional mechanic inspect the bar. The noise could be signaling a crack.

Stem/steerer tube junction. For threadless stems, simply tighten the bolt(s) on the stem's side, which should quiet the creak. For threaded stems, mark the stem height with a piece of tape. If you have brake levers with cables that run under handlebar tape, remove the front brake from the fork but leave the cable attached. Unscrew the threaded stem's expander bolt about four turns, then rap it sharply with a plastic mallet to free the plug. Pull the stem from the steerer tube, grease it, reinsert it to the tape, and snugly tighten the expander bolt after you align the stem with the front wheel.

Brake levers. On a road bike, if you hear creaking when you stand with your hands on the brake hoods, the levers may be a bit loose. Snug them with the appropriate allen wrench or screwdriver.

Seat Bleats

You're not likely to associate the seat with peculiar noises, but you might hear a snap or creak that emanates from the saddle though it seems to come from someplace else. Apply spray lube along the interface between the rails and seatpost clamp, and at the points where the rails enter the seat's plastic shell. Make sure the seatpost fixing bolt and the frame binder bolt are both greased and tight.

Bad Vibes

Puzzling buzzing could mean your bike has one of these problems.

The water bottle is vibrating in its cage. To fix a metal cage, carefully bend it inward to hold the bottle tighter. If it's a plastic cage, wrap electrical tape around contact points with the bottle to snug the fit. Also, check the tightness of the bolts holding the cage to the frame.

The brake cable housing is vibrating against the handlebar, stem, frame, reflectors, or other housing. While riding, touch different sections of housing to locate the buzzing. By shortening, rerouting, or taping the housing, you can eliminate the noise. On bikes with runs of bare brake cable, the cable can clatter against the frame, especially on bumps. Visit the bike shop to get miniature rubber donuts that fit around the cable. One every 5 to 6 inches should do the trick.

   The pump has loose parts or is vibrating against the frame. Check the pump for tightness. Stuff an old helmet pad into the handle to silence the rebound spring. If everything is in order, reposition the pump on the pump peg. Still buzzing? Wrap tape around the pump or frame where there's contact.

   The brake pads are squealing. This irritating and embarrassing noise isn't much of a mystery—you hear it almost every time you use the brakes. The cause is pad vibration, which can be remedied by toeing the pads so their front ends contact the rim first. On some brakes, you do this by slipping an adjustable wrench over each brake arm and gently bending it. Other brakes have toe-in adjusters built in. If the brakes still squeal, the pads may have hardened with age, in which case you should replace them; or you may need to use emery cloth or fine steel wool to sand rubber deposits from the rim sidewalls.

Rattles and Jingles

It can be tough to find the source of these, but here are some suspects.

   Seatbag. A loose under-saddle seatbag can bang against the seatpost, so secure it firmly. Inside, wrap loose, jingly tools with rubber bands or a rag.

   Coins. Loose change in a jersey pocket can drive your riding partners batty. Try using a change purse or putting the coins in a plastic bag wrapped with a rubber band.

   Lockrings. This classic mystery jingle occurs on noncartridge bottom brackets when the bottom bracket lockring loosens and rides on the axle. Immediate attention is required, or this dainty noise will be followed by the sound of bearings and races being pulverized. You also hear tinkling when dustcaps loosen and bounce on the hub axles. Push them back into place with your thumbs. Check the cassette, too. If the lockring is loose, the cogs will rattle and the derailleur won't shift well.

   Loose fittings. Anything that's attached to the frame—pump, computer, water bottle cage, racks, fenders—can rattle or vibrate loose. Regularly check all fittings, and use tape to deaden noise caused by metal-to-metal contact.

   Loose headset. Shudders and clunks when you ride over bumps mean the headset is loose. You can merely tighten it using the proper size wrenches, but if it hasn't been overhauled in awhile, you'd better take this opportunity to check the condition of the bearings, too. Depending on which type of headset you have, consult chapter 22 or 23.

Thumps

These are usually felt rather than heard, and they occur whether you're pedaling or coasting. Wheels are the cause. Check for these problems.

Unround rims. Spin each wheel and observe the rim where it passes the brake pads. True out-of-round rims; replace bent ones.

Rim blips. These bulges in the sidewall cause thumping during braking. They result from hitting an object, such as the edge of a pothole or rock, with underinflated tires. Blips can be carefully squeezed with Channellock pliers that have parallel jaws, or you could press them out with a bench vise. If you go too far and create an indent, consider it the lesser of two evils. If your wheel thumps badly as the seam in the rim passes through the brake pads, take it to a pro mechanic for an evaluation.

Bulging tires. A tire with a damaged casing looks like a snake after a good meal. A blowout is inevitable, so you must replace the tire right away. If this problem suddenly develops during a ride, release some air to reduce stress on the casing, and be very careful riding home. If you notice a bulge after installing a tire, it's defective or the bead is improperly seated. Inspect the sidewalls and tread for lumps, bulges, or tears. If there are none, spin the wheel and watch the bead line that's molded into the sidewalls. It appears just above the rim on both sides. Slight up-and-down fluctuations are normal, but if the line dips out of sight or hops significantly, deflate the tube and massage the tire at the trouble spots. Push the valve stem into the tire, then pull it down to make sure the tube isn't trapped under the edge and lifting the tire. Inflate halfway, check to see that everything looks right, then pump to full pressure.

5
Wash and Polish

A clean bike looks nice, but that's only one of several benefits of keeping your machine sparkling. You'll also find that it is easier to work on, is smoother to ride, lasts longer, and holds its value. Cleaning also helps you find faulty parts or frame defects before they become troublesome. That's an important reason that team mechanics wash their racers' bikes after each event.

Of course, you don't need to clean your bike after every ride unless you mountain bike on muddy trails. Usually, you can just spruce it up with a moist rag or a little cleaner wax. But several times a year, particularly after a spell of foul-weather riding, you should wash your bike thoroughly. (By the way, never wipe off dirt or caked mud with a dry rag or brush, because this will scratch the paint.)

Equipment and Supplies

Washing a bike is a lot like washing a car. You'll need a hose, two buckets, sponges, rags, and brushes of various sizes. Mark the brushes with colored tape so you can keep those used on greasy parts separate from those used on the rest of the bike. This way, you won't mistakenly smudge grease on your tires, handlebar tape, or saddle.

A repair stand is helpful because you need to remove both wheels for thorough cleaning. It's handy to have a portable stand that you can take outside. Don't turn the bike upside down for cleaning, as doing so will cause fluids to run into the headset and other parts, washing away lubrication and possibly causing internal tube corrosion.

In addition, you need detergent and a solvent (degreaser). Pedro's USA and Finish Line are companies that make various bike-care products, including biodegradable solvents that are a lot safer than old standbys such as diesel fuel and kerosene. The spray polish from Pedro's USA, called Bike Lust, won't cause unsightly buildup in tight places the way that car waxes can. In general, waxing the frame isn't essential, but it does make subsequent cleanings easier. Simichrome, available at bike shops and auto parts stores, is an abrasive paste that restores the luster of aluminum alloy.

It's possible to clean the chain quite well without removing it. Several companies make solvent reservoirs that snap around a section of chain and scrub it with brushes as you hand pedal. If you are good about keeping to a schedule of regular chain maintenance, a snap-on chain cleaner should make the chain as clean as new. However, if the chain is covered with sludge, you should remove it and let it soak in solvent. For this, you'll need a chain rivet extractor (and a replacement Shimano chain rivet if yours is a Shimano Hyperglide chain), a shallow pan, and a toothbrush to remove loosened deposits. It's smart to put on goggles and rubber gloves before working with solvent.

Never use a product such as Armor All on bike tires, because it will make them slippery and could also impair braking.

Step-by-Step Cleaning

Once you have the materials gathered, you're ready to clean your bike. Here's how.

Put the bike on the stand and remove the wheels. If you plan to clean the chain without removing it, put the rear wheel's quick-release skewer or a long screwdriver through one of the triangular holes in the rear dropouts, through the chain, then through the opposite triangular hole. This holds the chain so you can turn the crankset without the chain scraping the right chainstay. Otherwise, remove the chain and put it in the pan of solvent.

Fill two buckets with water. Put a good household detergent in one and a mixture of detergent and solvent in the other. The detergent is for washing the bike. The mixture is for cleaning greasy parts.

Install the snap-on chain cleaner. If you don't have one but still want to clean the chain without removing it, spray it with solvent. Also apply solvent to the derailleurs, chainrings, and cogs. Don't use too much. Let it soak in. (Avoid spraying solvent or water directly at the hubs, headset, cassette body, pedals, and bottom bracket. Spraying them could contaminate bearing grease or wash it away, leading to wear. Always squirt from above or below rather than from the side.)

Turn the crankset to clean the chain. If you don't have a snap-on chain cleaner, use a stiff brush dipped in the detergent/solvent mixture to scrub the top and bottom of the chain as it passes over the screwdriver. It may take several revolutions of the chain to get it clean. Continue hand pedaling and scrubbing, periodically dipping the brush in the mixture.

Brush the derailleurs and chainrings with the mixture.

Wash the rest of the bike. Use the detergent bucket and a sponge. A small, narrow brush is handy for hard-to-reach spots (see photo on page 22).

Lay the rear wheel on the mixture bucket and brush the cogs. Be careful not to get any of the fluid on the rim or tire or into the bearings under the smallest and largest cogs. Slip a rag between each pair of cogs and slide it back and forth like you're shining shoes, removing grime and excess solvent.

Wash both wheels. Hold them over the detergent bucket. Use sponges and brushes on the tires, rims, spokes, and hubs.

Rinse everything. Hold a hose or bucket of clean water above the bike and let a soft stream flow over the frame and parts. Do the same to the wheels.

Dry the bike with soft rags. Use separate rags for the drivetrain and frame and wheels.

Clean any rubber deposits from the sidewalls of both rims. Do this gently with fine steel wool or emery cloth.

Apply polish to all painted and chrome parts. Or use wax, if desired. Follow the product's directions. Use Simichrome to polish aluminum parts if they're dull with oxidation.

Lubricate everything. Use a spray lube with a thin nozzle tube to spritz the brake and derailleur pivots and all points where cables enter or exit housings and touch guides or stops. Wipe off any excess. Also lubricate the chain if it remained on the bike during this cleaning.

Reassemble the bike. If you removed the chain to soak it, finish cleaning it with a brush. Wipe it down well, hang it to dry, apply lubrication, then wipe it again before you reinstall it.

Pack your wet-weather gear. It's bound to rain on your next ride.

PART TWO

Tires
and Wheels

6

Clincher Tire Repair

A flat tire is one of those nuisances that always seem to occur at the most inopportune time. But it doesn't have to ruin your ride if you know how to make the repair quickly. Some riders are so efficient that they get pedaling again in less than five minutes. The procedure is easy to master.

Because patching tires with highway tar is virtually impossible, fast flat fixing starts with having the right supplies. Your seatbag should include a spare tube of the correct size and valve type, two tire levers, a patch kit (for the inevitable second puncture), a piece of canvas or denim to "boot" a large hole in the tire, and change to call for help if you suffer a blowout that can't be repaired. You also need a tire pump or CO_2 cartridge for inflation. Make sure it fits your valve type, either Schrader (as found on auto tires) or presta (the narrow European style).

The procedure described below is for a rear flat because rear-wheel removal is more complicated than front-wheel removal. Actual tube replacement is the same for both wheels.

Remove the Wheel and Tube

Before rolling to a stop, shift to the smallest cog. If you don't have time, hand pedal and shift after you get off. This moves the derailleur as far from under the wheel as possible. If there's a peg on the inside of the right seatstay, lift the chain onto it with a tire lever or your finger.

Spread the brake pads by whatever means provided, which may be unhooking a cable or using a quick-release on the brake or its lever. Open the hub quick-release by pivoting its lever.

To remove the wheel, lift the bike by the seat with one hand while pushing the wheel forward and down with the other. If the chain clings to the cogs, shake the wheel to free it. Once the wheel is out, lay the bike on its left side so the drivetrain isn't on the ground.

Remove the valve cap and deflate the tube completely by depressing the spring-loaded center pin on a Schrader valve or by unscrewing and depressing the pin on a presta valve.

Insert the flat, spoonlike end of one tire lever between the tire bead and the rim about 2 inches from the valve. Lift up the bead by pulling the lever down and hooking it to a spoke.

Insert the second lever under the same bead about 4 inches farther from the valve. Pull the lever down, prying off more of the bead. You should now be able to slide the second lever along the rim to free one side of the tire. If the bead is too tight, hold the dislodged portion and move several inches farther along with the second lever. You don't need to unseat the other bead from the rim.

Starting opposite the valve, pull the inner tube from the tire. Then pull out the valve stem.

Find the Puncture

To locate the puncture, inflate the tube and listen for a hiss. Water or saliva rubbed on a leak will bubble to confirm that you've found the spot.

Hold the valve stem next to the rim's valve hole so you can match the hole in the tube to the tire. Look closely at the tread and casing to find the hole or cut. You may see a shard of glass or another sharp object lodged in the tread. Pick it out, then double-check by carefully feeling around the inside circumference of the tire.

If the tire has a hole larger than $\frac{1}{8}$ inch or a cut in the sidewall, you must cover it, or the new tube will squeeze through and blow out. Use your boot material or an appropriate size patch from your repair kit. In a pinch, scour the roadside for a tough piece of paper or use a folded dollar bill (it's made of linen). Place the material across the hole as you install the spare tube. If you inflate only to 75 percent of maximum pressure, you should be able to ride home safely.

Install the Spare Tube

Inflate the spare tube just enough to unflatten it. Insert the valve stem through the rim. Carefully tuck the entire tube into the tire so there are no kinks or wrinkles. Begin working the bead onto the rim, starting at the valve. Use your hands instead of tire levers so you don't accidentally cause another puncture by pinching the tube.

The last section of bead will become tight and hard to get onto the rim. Deflate the tube completely to minimize its size, then use your thumbs or palms to force the bead into place (see photo). Push the valve stem into the tire to ensure that the tube isn't trapped under the bead, then pull it out firmly.

Inflate the tube to about half of the pressure listed on the tire sidewall. Hold the hub axle in your hands so you can spin the wheel and watch the bead line that's molded into each side of the tire. It should appear just above the rim. If it bulges up, let out the air and work that section with your hands to get the tube out from under the bead. If it dips below, continue inflating to maximum recommended pressure and you'll probably hear it pop into place. Spin the wheel and eye the line again to make sure. If a section of bead refuses to seat, deflate the tire and rub a little saliva or soap on the bead. This should make it seat when you try again.

Install the Wheel

Hold the bike upright by the seat or left seatstay with your left hand. Roll the wheel into place. Use your right hand to pull back the rear derailleur. Set the top run of chain onto the smallest cog (the position that the drivetrain was in before you removed the wheel). Set the bike down so the axle is positioned in front of the dropouts, then pull the wheel back into the slots.

Make sure the wheel is centered in the frame. A good indicator is equal distance between the tire and chainstays behind the bottom bracket.

Close the hub quick-release. The lever should require enough force to make an imprint on your palm. If necessary, turn the nut on the other end until the lever tightens firmly enough.

Close the brake release or reconnect the cable. Make sure the wheel spins without rubbing.

Pick up all of your gear and stow it in your seatbag or pockets.

Patching a Tube

On the road, it's easier and quicker to install a spare tube than to patch the punctured one. Carry the bad boy home and patch it later for use as a spare. Here's how.

Choose the right patch. Small round ones are for pinhole punctures, while oval patches fit the dual "snakebite" holes made by a rim pinch. Blowouts cause a large hole that usually can't be reliably patched.

Locate the puncture by putting air in the tube, then running it past your ear or lips to hear or feel the spot where air is escaping. Still can't find it? Put a section at a time in a sink full of water till you see the tell-tale bubbles. Once you have found the hole, draw an X across it with a ballpoint pen. This will stay visible during the repair.

Buff the area with sandpaper. This rough section needs to be a bit larger than the patch.

Apply a thin, even coat of glue to the buffed surface and give it a couple of minutes to dry. It will turn from shiny to dull.

Peel the foil backing from the patch and carefully apply the exposed rubber side to the glued area, pressing it firmly into place (you only get one chance). Some patches have foil on one side and cellophane on the other. The surface under the foil goes against the glue. It's smart to leave the cellophane on so the patch won't stick to the inside of the tire.

7

Wheel Truing

Truing bicycle wheels is not some arcane science reserved for professional bike mechanics, aerospace engineers, or the most technologically gifted among us. It requires only a basic understanding of the process, then some practice. It's worth learning because straight, evenly ten-

sioned wheels roll smoother, last longer, and allow tighter brake adjustment.

A good way to develop truing ability is to practice on an old wheel,
perhaps one that you don't even use. A bike shop may have a discarded
wheel that it will give to you, or you could buy one for next to nothing
at a garage sale. An ideal practice wheel will have significant wobbles,
but make sure that the spoke nipples aren't frozen by rust and that the
rim hasn't been bent by an accident. The sidewalls should also be free of
dents or bulges. These problems make truing difficult or impossible for
even the best wheelsmith.

Tools

The most important truing tool is a wrench for turning the spoke nipples. Nipples come in slightly different sizes, but you needn't worry
about this if you purchase a multisize spoke wrench or a set of individual spoke wrenches in a range of sizes.

Truing can be done with the wheel in the bike, but it's much easier
and more exact if you use a truing stand (see photo), which lets you
spin the wheel and correct the rim for wobbles as it passes adjustable
reference arms. Truing stands are available from bike shops and mail-
order catalogs, beginning at about $50.

In this discussion, it's assumed that you are using such a stand. (Otherwise, hang or support your bike so the wheel that you are truing is off the ground. Use the brake pads for reference points. If the wheel is so out of true that it cannot spin past the pads, open the brake quick-release to provide extra room.)

Inspection

Damaged wheel components make truing difficult. For instance, sometimes the corners of the nipples, which are made of brass or aluminum, become rounded. This prevents you from getting a good grip with the spoke wrench. As the nipple gets tight, the wrench starts slipping. Damaged nipples should be replaced one at a time before you start truing. Corroded nipples may not turn at all. You can try applying penetrating oil, but usually the best solution is to rebuild the wheel with new spokes, assuming the rim and hub are worth salvaging.

Certain types of damage mean the rim should be replaced. When the rim is bent laterally or out of round by a severe impact, or when it has numerous dents or bulges in its sidewalls, spoke tension adjustments do little good. Ride quality and braking will remain poor.

Truing Procedure

The goal is to make the wheel true laterally (no wobbles) and vertically (no hops or flat spots). Lateral truing is easier and, in most cases, more important.

Spin the wheel slowly. Watch for lateral movement relative to the adjustable reference arms. When learning to true, it's helpful to mark the wobbles by holding a felt-tip pen against one of the reference arms. This helps you see the sections of rim you need to work on.

Wiggle each spoke. Find any that are looser (or, less commonly, tighter) than the others. Mark them with the pen or pieces of electrical tape. It's likely that these abnormal spokes are near your rim marks.

Tighten spokes. Rotate the wheel so a loose spoke is at the truing stand's reference arms. Turn the nipple counterclockwise one-half turn at a time until it feels as tight as the neighboring spokes when you wiggle it. Repeat for the other loose spokes.

To prevent getting confused and turning a spoke nipple the wrong way, always work at the same location—near the stand's arms at the bottom of the wheel. In this position, as you look at the nipple from above, counterclockwise turns tighten the spoke and clockwise turns loosen it.

A well-built wheel is strong and durable because its spokes are evenly tensioned. While this is difficult to measure without a special, relatively expensive tool called a spoke tensiometer, adequate strength can be achieved by developing a feel for firm tension. After finding and tightening all loose spokes (or loosening overly tight ones), you should notice that the wheel spins with fewer wobbles. Simply equalizing spoke tension has made it straighter.

Important: A front hub is symmetrical, so a front wheel's spokes are equally tensioned to center the rim between the hub flanges. In a rear wheel, however, the spokes radiating from the right hub flange must be tighter than those on the left. This higher tension pulls the rim to the right relative to the flanges, which are offset because of the width of the cassette on the right side. With the rim centered on the axle rather than the flanges, the wheel centers in the frame. Still, the spokes in each flange should be equally tensioned among themselves.

Remove the remaining lateral movement. This takes patience. Always adjust nipples one-half turn at a time, then spin the wheel to check progress. It may look like little happens, but keep working and the wheel will improve.

Every wheel has right- and left-side spokes. At the rim, the spokes alternate to either side of the hub. If you need to move a portion of rim to the left, you can tighten spokes leading from it to the left flange, loosen spokes leading to the right flange, or do a little of each. Always check for relatively loose or tight spokes at the wobble, and take this into account when deciding what to do. Usually, abnormalities correspond to the wobble in the rim, and correcting them results in quick alignment. This may require adjusting only two to four nipples.

True the largest wobble (the longest mark on the rim), then move to the next one. For instance, if the mark is on the right side of the rim, that part of the rim needs to move to the left. If the spokes feel evenly tensioned, loosen the right-side spokes in this area one-half turn and tighten the left-side spokes one-half turn. Check the result.

Try to tighten or loosen several spokes at a time, and never adjust just one spoke unless it is obviously improperly tensioned. Always strive to create or maintain equal tension during truing. Continue working until all wobbles are gone.

Eliminate vertical movement (put a wheel into "round"). This may be more difficult with a used rim. Spin the wheel and look for up or down movement relative to the reference arms. (Unlike for lateral truing, the tire and tube must be removed for this procedure.) Again, mark the problem spots. If the rim moves inward toward the hub (a "flat spot"), slightly loosen four consecutive spokes in that area. If the rim moves away from the hub (a "hop"), tighten four spokes in that area. Why an even number? Because this keeps left- and right-side spoke tension equal so the rim isn't pulled out of true. When you're done rounding, recheck lateral movement and touch up if necessary. Keep in mind that it's normally not possible (or essential) to make a wheel perfectly round.

Also, exact vertical or lateral alignment will be impossible on a beat-up practice wheel. When it's as good as possible, have a friend mess up spoke tension at random so you can start over again. It won't be long before you feel confident enough to work on your own wheels. In fact, when you're skilled enough to true a raggedy old wheel, touching up good ones is easy.

8
Spoke Replacement

Good-quality spokes in well-built, properly tensioned wheels can do their job for years without a whimper. Someday, though, a spoke will snap. The wheel will immediately go out of true and complicate the ride you're on, but don't despair. Replacing a broken spoke is an easy procedure.

For some cosmic reason, spokes seem to break when you're farthest from your destination. Telltale signs are the sound of the spoke snapping or beating against the stays or fork blades on every wheel revolution. You may also feel the wheel twitching. If you don't have a spoke wrench in your tool kit, follow these steps.

Immediately stop and unscrew the threaded end of the broken spoke from the nipple. Spokes usually break at the bend, leaving them swinging in the wheel. If the nipple won't yield, wrap the broken spoke

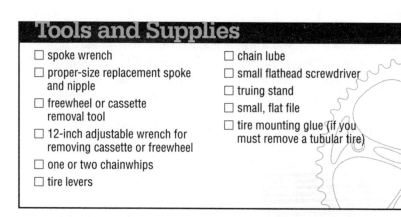

Tools and Supplies

- ☐ spoke wrench
- ☐ proper-size replacement spoke and nipple
- ☐ freewheel or cassette removal tool
- ☐ 12-inch adjustable wrench for removing cassette or freewheel
- ☐ one or two chainwhips
- ☐ tire levers
- ☐ chain lube
- ☐ small flathead screwdriver
- ☐ truing stand
- ☐ small, flat file
- ☐ tire mounting glue (if you must remove a tubular tire)

around an adjoining spoke to prevent it from snagging something and causing further damage.

Open the quick-release lever on the appropriate brake to allow the wobbly rim to spin without hitting the pads.

Gingerly ride home. Excessive mileage or impacts on a wheel weakened by a broken spoke can permanently damage the rim.

If you do have a spoke wrench, loosen a spoke on each side of the broken one until the rim becomes reasonably true again. This will improve braking and reduce the risk of permanent rim damage as you ride home. Self-reliant cyclists with spare spokes and proper tools can follow the rest of the instructions for a complete roadside repair.

Spokes and Other Stuff

Most bike shops stock a full range of spoke lengths. Spokes come in 1- or 2-mm increments and several different styles and gauges (thicknesses). For these reasons, it's always advisable to take your ailing wheel with you when spoke shopping. Next best is the broken spoke itself and exact information about the lacing pattern, hub and rim brand or model, and the number of spokes the wheel requires. Otherwise, it's impossible for the shop to determine the style and length you need. Once you find the correct replacement spoke, buy several so you're ready for the next break. (Once one spoke snaps for no apparent reason in an older wheel, fatigue is the likely cause and others may follow. Rebuilding the wheel with all new spokes will lessen hassle and increase safety.) Also, buy a spoke wrench if you don't have one that precisely fits the nipples in your wheels.

If a spoke breaks on the cog side of the rear wheel (the most common location), you will also need a removal tool for the freewheel or cassette lockring, plus one or two chainwhips. Check chapter 17 for the instructions on how to remove cogs. If the broken spoke is on the rear hub's left side, you can usually replace it with the cogs in place.

Out with the Old and In with the New

To properly install a spoke, remove the tire, tube, and rim strip (or tubular tire) from the wheel. Inspect the rim for dents, cracks, or other damage around the broken spoke. Have the wheel evaluated by a professional mechanic if there is anything suspicious.

Remove the broken spoke. Lube the threads of the new spoke. Slide the spoke through the hub flange from the proper direction (opposite to the two adjacent spokes). If you're inserting from outside to inside, gently curve the spoke's threaded end toward the rim in order to keep it from being obstructed by the spokes on the opposite side (or by the cogs, if working on a rear wheel).

Lace the spoke to the rim. Simply imitate the pattern of a spoke that enters the flange from the same direction as the spoke you're working with.

Screw on the new spoke nipple. It's okay if three or four spoke threads are still exposed on the hub side of the nipple when it's finger tight, but if any threads protrude on the tire side, the spoke is too long and you need to exchange it for one that's sufficiently shorter. First, double-check that you've laced it right.

Truing

To true the wheel, first place it in a truing stand or reinstall it on the bike.

When truing on the bike, pivot the brake so one pad works as a reference point. If you didn't loosen a spoke on each side of the broken one, you can usually true the wheel by simply tightening the new spoke nipple until that portion of the rim runs straight.

If you did loosen the two adjacent spokes, you'll have to tighten them as well as the new spoke to make the wheel true and round. Start by tightening the new spoke nipple until the rim runs straight. Then pluck all three spokes and compare their tone to others on the wheel. (Remember, spokes on a rear wheel's cog side are tighter and have a higher tone than those on the left side.) Tighten the two loosened spokes and the new spoke one-quarter turn each while comparing tones. Don't worry about achieving concert quality—just make them sound similar.

Spin the wheel to inspect your work. If everything looks good laterally, check for roundness. If there is a flat spot or hop at the new spoke, correct it using the procedure in chapter 7.

Check inside the rim. File down the end of any spoke that is protruding from the nipple. Reinstall the rim strip, tire, and tube (or reglue a tubular tire). If you hear a couple of pings from the wheel as you ride away, that's merely the sound of the spokes seating. Touch up trueness, if necessary, after a ride or two.

9
Rim Replacement

Many home mechanics consider wheel building an art that's best left to the pros. One reason for their trepidation is the difficulty of lacing spokes. But did you know that there's a way to skip this step entirely? If the spokes are sound and an identical replacement rim (same brand and model) is available, you can rebuild the wheel simply by removing the nipples rather than disassembling the spokes. Thus, you needn't know a thing about the intricacies of lacing.

Inspection

Spokes begin breaking as a wheel becomes old and fatigued. Usually, they snap at the sharp bend into the hub flange. You can't see this problem ahead of time, but if a spoke or two breaks at this point, it's a pretty safe bet that more will follow. You're better off replacing all of the spokes than risking breakdowns on rides and adding new spokes piecemeal.

Other signs of a problem are more visible. Squeeze each pair of crossed spokes so they separate, then look at the junction where they've been in contact. If there is a deep groove, the spokes should be replaced. Also replace rusty spokes or those with nipples frozen by corrosion.

All of these problems mean the wheel isn't a good candidate for simple rim replacement. If the hub is worth saving, the wheel should be professionally rebuilt with a new rim and spokes. Otherwise, simply buy a new wheel. But if the only thing wrong is a damaged rim, you can go ahead with this procedure.

Rim Choice

Spoke lengths vary in millimeter increments. The proper size for any given wheel depends on several factors, including rim design. Thus, when purchasing a replacement rim, you should take your wheel to the shop in order to get the same brand, model, and number of spoke holes. If an identical rim isn't available, ask a shop mechanic to find one with the same dimensions. The mechanic can do this by using a spoke chart.

If a different rim is to be used, check its spoke hole orientation. Most rims have offset holes, meaning that every other hole is closer to one side of the rim. Lay the new rim atop the old wheel with the valve holes aligned. Check the spoke hole to the right of the valve on each rim. The offset should be to the same side.

Often, you'll be replacing the rim because it's been badly warped in a crash. This condition is called pretzeled or taco'd. It can be difficult to transfer the spokes unless you make the rim straighter before you begin.

Start by loosening all of the spokes so none are under firm tension. Spin the wheel and note where the rim is badly warped and in which direction it needs to be bent. Place the worst section against your knee and pull it into shape as if you were breaking kindling.

Tools and Supplies

- ☐ replacement spokes (if necessary)
- ☐ tire levers
- ☐ cassette or freewheel removal tool (if necessary)
- ☐ 12-inch adjustable wrench (if necessary)
- ☐ one or two chain whips (if necessary)
- ☐ new rim
- ☐ spoke wrench
- ☐ electrical tape
- ☐ small flathead screwdriver
- ☐ linseed oil or spoke thread lubricant/adhesive (available at shops)
- ☐ truing stand
- ☐ felt-tip pen
- ☐ dishing gauge
- ☐ spoke tensiometer

An alternative is the slam method. Do this with the tire inflated. Locate the worst section, then hold the wheel with both hands and strike this section against the floor. Start gently and increase the strength of the blows as necessary. Continue around the rim until it's fairly straight.

Spoke Transfer

Remove the tire, tube, and rim strip (or tubular tire). If any spokes need to be replaced in the rear wheel, see chapter 17 for instructions on removing the cassette or freewheel.

Loosen all of the nipples, but don't remove them.

Replace any damaged spokes, being careful to duplicate their orientation in the hub (head in or head out) and the way they weave past other spokes.

Align the valve hole of the new rim with that of the old one, then tape them together in about six places (see photo).

Starting next to the valve hole, transfer each spoke to the new rim. Use a screwdriver on the head of the nipple (inside the rim) to speed the process. Engage the nipples about two turns.

Put a drop of oil on the spoke threads and in each nipple pocket of the new rim. Linseed oil is favored by many pro wheelbuilders because it dries to a tacky consistency that keeps nipples from vibrating loose. Or purchase some spoke thread lubricant/adhesive at a shop.

Truing

This is the important part, so take your time. Don't add too much spoke tension until the new rim is round and true. It's easy to be overzealous. Proceed in half-turns and frequently check progress by spinning the wheel.

Put the wheel in your truing stand. If you don't have one, put it into your bike. Prop the bike so you can spin the wheel.

Tighten each nipple equally with a screwdriver. To be certain they're consistent, count the number of spoke threads still showing. If the rear wheel uses spokes that are all the same size (this is the way most factory-built wheels are set up), leave three threads exposed on all left-side spokes and no threads showing on right-side spokes. This will offset the wheel relative to the cassette on the right side. If the wheel has shorter spokes on the right side (this is the way most hand-built wheels are set up), tighten all spokes to the same thread.

Check trueness. Spin the wheel and viewing the rim's position relative to the truing stand's adjustable reference arms or the brake pads. You may find it helpful to hold a felt-tip pen next to the rim to mark out-of-true spots as they pass. Follow the lateral-truing procedure described in chapter 7. Remember that tightening and loosening alternating spokes will ensure that the wheel remains round. The wheel should still have only minimal spoke tension when you finish this step.

Check for vertical movement (roundness). Spin the wheel. For reference, use the arms of the truing stand or place a pencil across the brake pads and view the rim as it passes. If a section of rim is high, tighten four spokes in that area (two on each side) one-quarter turn apiece, check progress, then tighten more if necessary. If the rim is low, loosen spokes. At this stage, try to loosen rather than tighten, and always work in pairs.

Repeat steps 3 and 4. Do this until the rim is true and round.

Squeeze pairs of spokes gently to seat the nipples. Use both hands (one on each side of the wheel).

Add tension. For a front wheel, tighten every spoke one-half turn. For a rear wheel, tighten the right-side spokes one-half turn and the left-hand spokes one-quarter turn. Start each pass at the valve hole so you know where to stop.

Check wheel dish. Dish is correct when the rim is centered between the outside faces of the axle locknuts. This ensures that the wheel will align with the center of the frame. Follow the manufacturer's instructions when using a dishing gauge. Otherwise, flip the wheel over in the truing stand (or frame) periodically and check the rim's distance from each side. It should be the same regardless of wheel orientation. To alter dish, tighten all spokes on one side of the wheel one-quarter turn to pull the rim in that direction. Check and repeat as necessary.

Continue adding tension. Keep squeezing spokes and adjusting for trueness and roundness until the proper tension is achieved. A spoke tensiometer is the most accurate way to verify this, so you may want to take the wheel to a shop mechanic if you don't have one. Otherwise, squeeze spokes and compare their tension to those in a well-built wheel, or pluck spokes and compare their tone. Remember that left-side spokes in a rear wheel will not be as tight as those on the right side.

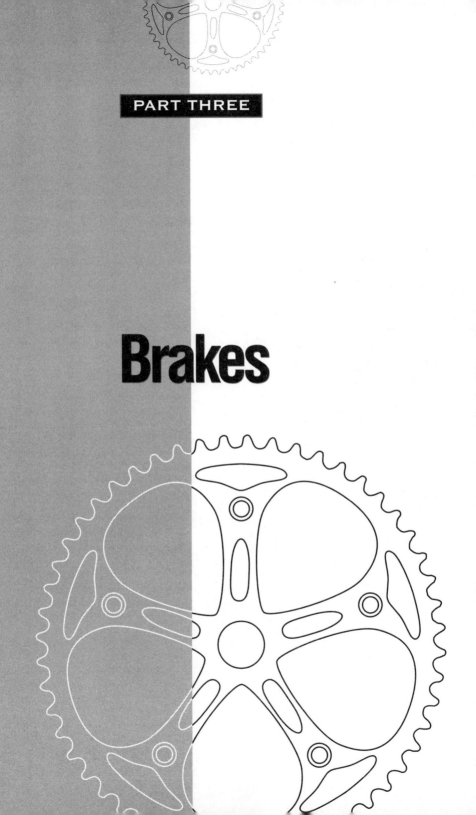

PART THREE

Brakes

10

Sidepull Brakes

Sidepull, or caliper, brakes come with various means of adjustment. The brake style and technique described here are probably the most common. Some new designs have a small adjustment screw in one of the arms. Simply turning it in or out centers the pads with the rim.

Check hubs and spokes. Before adjusting brakes, check hub bearing adjustment by grasping each rim and trying to move it laterally in the frame. If there's play, remove the wheels and use cone wrenches to remedy it. Wiggle each spoke to check tension. If any are loose, tighten as necessary with a spoke wrench until the wheels are true. Make sure both wheels are centered in the frame.

Grease cables. Remove the cable end caps, loosen the cable anchor bolts, and pull the cables from the calipers. Slide housing sections so you can grease the parts of cable that are normally covered. Replace a cable that's rusted or frayed and housing that's cracked.

Align and lube levers. On a drop handlebar, hold a straightedge underneath each lower section so it extends forward toward the brake levers. It should just touch the lever tips. Reposition the levers if necessary. Make sure they are clamped tight to the bar. Hold each lever handle down and lightly spray the internal pivots. If necessary, retape the bar and replace cracked or torn lever hoods.

Replace old or worn brake pads. Pads can harden with age, and they're too worn if grooves no longer appear on the braking surfaces. Position new pads to contact the rim squarely, then tighten. Toe in all pads slightly by gingerly bending the caliper arms with an adjustable wrench or by pivoting the conical washers on brake pads that are so equipped. You have it right when the fronts of the pads strike the rims first as the brakes are applied. Toe-in shouldn't be so much that it prevents the rest of the pad from making contact as braking pressure is increased.

Lubricate. Unscrew the cable adjustment barrels, grease their threads, screw them down, then back off two turns. Spray or drip lube on the caliper arm pivots, brake spring tips (behind the arms), quick-releases, and anchor bolts. In other words, if it moves, lube it. Wipe away any excess. Check the snugness of the nut or bolt that holds each brake to the frame.

Check center pivots. On brakes with two nuts on the front of a central pivot bolt, check for looseness by gently pushing and pulling the arms fore and aft. If there's play, remove it with the appropriate two wrenches (see photo). Don't make this adjustment so tight that the brakes can't snap open easily from spring tension, but do make sure the nuts are tight against each other so they stay in place.

Attach cables. Apply the third-hand tool to hold one brake closed with pads against the rim. Thread its cable through the adjustment barrel and anchor bolt, then grasp the end with pliers. Snap the lever a few times to remove all slack and make sure everything is seated. Tighten the anchor bolt and install the end cap. Repeat for the other brake.

Test the system. Squeeze the brake levers to the bar repeatedly to stretch the cable and see that everything is tight. If necessary, remove slack through the cable anchor bolt as in step 7. When you're done, there should be ⅛-inch clearance between the front of each pad and the rim. Too tight? Just turn the adjustment barrel to let out some cable. To make the pads equidistant from the rim, slip a cone wrench on the center bolt flats behind the caliper arms and pivot the brake. Also check for deposits on rims that can inhibit smooth braking. Apply acetone to a rag and clean all sidewalls thoroughly. Avoid getting any on the tires (if they're installed).

Tools and Supplies

- ☐ repair stand
- ☐ cone wrenches
- ☐ spoke wrench
- ☐ cables and housing
- ☐ cable cutters
- ☐ grease
- ☐ straightedge
- ☐ spray or drip lube
- ☐ handlebar tape
- ☐ lever hoods
- ☐ adjustable wrench

- ☐ brake pads
- ☐ rags
- ☐ 3-, 4-, 5-, and 6-mm allen wrenches
- ☐ 8-, 9-, and 10-mm combination wrenches
- ☐ third-hand tool
- ☐ needle-nose pliers
- ☐ cable end caps
- ☐ acetone
- ☐ sandpaper or emery cloth

Take a test ride. Or, buff lightly with fine sandpaper or emery cloth and apply the brakes several times. Increase pad toe-in a smidgen to get rid of persistent squealing.

11

Cantilever Brakes

Some road bikes and many hybrids come with cantilever brakes, and you'd be hard-pressed to find an older mountain bike without them. Parallel-pull, or direct-pull, brakes have replaced cantilevers on many newer mountain bikes, so they're discussed in chapter 12.

Because wet and muddy off-road conditions are tough on cantilevers, they need frequent maintenance. In fact, pads can wear away during just one long gritty ride that has a good deal of braking. You need to keep your cantis in top shape to enhance control and safety.

Inspect wheels. With the bike in a repair stand, spin the wheels and examine them for trueness and roundness. Wiggle them laterally to feel for play in the hub bearings. If there is any, see chapter 20 for instructions of how to eliminate it. If necessary, true the wheels and adjust the hubs. Slide your thumbs or fingers between the rim and the seatstays or chainstays in the rear and between the rim and the fork blades in the front to tell if the wheels are centered in the frame. If necessary, loosen the hub quick-release, center the wheel, and retighten. Clean the rim sidewalls with acetone, being careful not to get any on the tires.

Examine cables. Squeeze the pads to the rim with your hand and unhook the end of the transverse cable from each brake. (This is the short cable that passes over the wheel to connect the two arms.) Inspect all cables and housings for binding, rusting, fraying, or cracking. If necessary, cut off the cable end, loosen the anchor bolt, and extract the damaged housing or cable and replace it. Use old housing sections to size replacements. Grease the head of the new cable where it fits into the lever as well as any sections that will be inside housing. Apply lube to the anchor bolt threads. Don't trim cables or tighten anchor bolts yet.

Align and lube brake levers. Flat-handlebar lever placement should result in straight wrists during braking. The lever tips shouldn't protrude beyond the end of the bar. Make sure the levers are tight. Lubricate the pivot points and adjustment barrels. Screw the latter in all the way, then back out two turns. To position brake levers on drop bars, see chapter 10.

Move each brake arm through its full range. If one binds, remove it from the frame by unscrewing the center bolt with a 5- or 6-mm allen

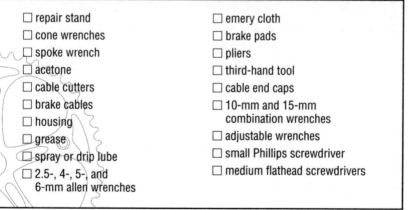

Tools and Supplies

- ☐ repair stand
- ☐ cone wrenches
- ☐ spoke wrench
- ☐ acetone
- ☐ cable cutters
- ☐ brake cables
- ☐ housing
- ☐ grease
- ☐ spray or drip lube
- ☐ 2.5-, 4-, 5-, and 6-mm allen wrenches

- ☐ emery cloth
- ☐ brake pads
- ☐ pliers
- ☐ third-hand tool
- ☐ cable end caps
- ☐ 10-mm and 15-mm combination wrenches
- ☐ adjustable wrenches
- ☐ small Phillips screwdriver
- ☐ medium flathead screwdrivers

wrench. Slide the arm off the post. Buff the post with emery cloth, grease it, and reinstall the arm and bolt. Try to move the arm fore and aft. If there's play, snug the center bolt. Don't overtighten, because that can cause binding.

Inspect brake pads. Most pads have wear indicators, usually grooves or notches. When these are nearly worn away, replace the pads. For pads without indicators, judge wear by checking depth. If a pad is less than 3-mm thick, replace it. Age and environmental conditions harden pads and reduce their effectiveness. Change pads that are more than two years old, even if they aren't completely worn.

Replace and align pads. Loosen the fixing nut so you can slide out the old pad and holder. Insert the new one and snug it in place. If the holder has an open end, that end faces the rear. Push the arm toward the rim to judge pad position. It must be toed-in slightly (the front end must touch the rim first when the brake is applied) to prevent squealing. The pad must also strike the rim perpendicularly so it won't dive underneath into the spokes or angle up into the tire. Many pads rest on concave washers that are used to set this position. You can also move pads in and out on the holders' posts to make them equidistant from the rim. To keep the adjustment from changing as you tighten the fixing nut, anchor the pad mount in place with an allen wrench or hold the pad with pliers.

Adjust cables. Hold the pads to the rim with a third-hand tool. The transverse cable attaches to, is clamped by, or passes through a triangular or round cable carrier on the main brake cable. For best performance, the transverse cable should be about one inch above the tire and should form a 90-degree angle with each brake arm. Keep the transverse cable taut and slide the carrier up or down the main cable. When the transverse cable looks right, tighten the carrier. Now pull the end of the transverse cable to remove slack, tighten its anchor bolt, and trim and cap both cables. (On some brakes, the carrier should not be tightened. It moves to the correct position when you tension the transverse cable.)

Test the system. Squeeze the brake levers hard to stretch new cables and see that nothing slips. Make any readjustments. If the brakes don't open quickly and evenly, increase spring tension. Some brakes have a small set screw or allen bolt in one arm. Turning this clockwise increases tension and moves the pad away from the rim, or vice versa. Other brakes are tensioned by loosening the arm's center bolt, turning

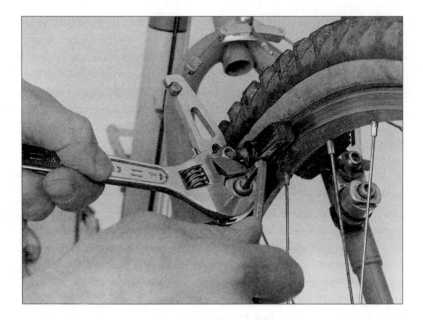

the spring holder with a wrench (away from the rim to add tension), and tightening the bolt to lock the adjustment (see photo).

12
Parallel-Pull Brakes

A new type of brake hit the market in the late 1990s and quickly supplanted regular cantilevers on better mountain bikes. These superior stoppers often go by the name V-brake, which is the tag Shimano hung on its version. Other companies make a similar product, so this book will use the term *parallel-pull brake*, which describes the cable path pulling directly on the arms. You may also hear it called direct pull.

With these brakes, the cable goes directly to a caliper arm rather than through a hanger as with cantilevers. The pads are mounted as close as possible to the frame. Also, the brake arms are extra long. These features improve power and control compared to regular cantis.

The advice below applies specifically to the ubiquitous Shimano brakes, but most of it works for the various competitors, too. One caution: All of these brakes require special parallel-pull–compatible levers that take up more cable than conventional levers. You won't get good performance without them.

These stoppers are so good that they work pretty well even when sloppily adjusted. But they're so easy to tune that you may as well dial them in. Here's how.

Check hubs for bearing play. Looseness can cause dragging brakes. Grab each wheel at the top and wiggle it sideways to feel for slop in the hub bearings. A trace is okay, but if a wheel actually moves sideways, remove it and adjust the bearings with cone wrenches. Working on the left side of a rear wheel or either side of a front, peel off the rubber dustcap (if so equipped) and place the appropriate cone wrenches on the cone and locknut. Hold the cone while turning the locknut counterclockwise to loosen it. Then turn the cone clockwise to remove play. Finish by snugging the locknut against the cone. The axle should now spin smoothly with no lateral movement.

Check rim condition. Round, true, and centered wheels stop best. Spin yours and inspect them for wobbles and hops. Find some? Remove the wheel, strip the tire and tube (this helps with truing and brake adjustment), and put it in your truing stand. If you don't have a stand, reinstall the wheel while the bike is held by a repair stand or otherwise suspended. True and round using the procedures described in chapter 7. Work until the wheel is as good as you can get it, then put it in the bike and make sure it's centered.

Orient the arms. For optimum power, the brake arms should be close to parallel. In Shimano models, you should be able to measure at least 39 mm from the edge of the right brake arm to the point where the cable "noodle" meets the holder when the brake is applied. To achieve this with different rim widths, each brake pad has thick and thin washers. Place the appropriate sizes between the pads and arms (keeping one inside and one outside). Then adjust the cable at the anchor bolt until you can measure at least 39 mm.

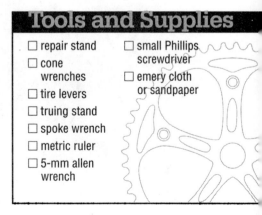

Tools and Supplies

- ☐ repair stand
- ☐ cone wrenches
- ☐ tire levers
- ☐ truing stand
- ☐ spoke wrench
- ☐ metric ruler
- ☐ 5-mm allen wrench
- ☐ small Phillips screwdriver
- ☐ emery cloth or sandpaper

Align the pads. It helps to release the spring on the side of the brake you're working on, because the other side will then pull the pad into the rim. Sight along the pad. It should strike the rim flat and be in line with the center of the rim. If necessary, loosen the 5-mm fixing nut, adjust the pad, tighten it securely, and reattach the spring. Then do the other side.

Center the brake. If one pad stays closer to the rim when you squeeze and release the lever, turn the small screw at the base of the arm (see photo). Clockwise turns increase spring tension, which moves the pad away from the rim. Counterclockwise turns have the opposite effect. Adjust the screw in one-half turn increments and snap the lever to check progress.

Silence squeaks. It can be challenging to quiet squeaky parallel-pull brakes. Try these tricks. Check the mounting bolts to ensure the arms are tight on the frame. If that's not the problem, then scuff the rim sidewalls with emery cloth or the sandpaper in your patch kit to break the glaze. Still noisy? Go for a ride and take along a 5-mm allen wrench; experiment with different brake pad toe-in angles to see if you can shut them up. (The fronts of the pads should touch the rim before the remainder comes into contact.) Didn't work? Try a different brand of brake pad. Howling anyway? Consider the purchase of a brake booster, which joins the two brake bosses and stiffens the system.

PART FOUR

Drivetrain

13

Chain Maintenance

The filth. The stench. The time. It's no wonder that many cyclists shun routine chain maintenance. Instead, they just add lube occasionally and replace the chain every year or so. This approach works, but the result will almost surely be premature wear to the chain, chainrings, and cogs. These parts will need to be replaced sooner to keep the drivetrain from skipping. A grimy chain also makes it messier to work on a bike or transport it. The best solution is regular maintenance. It's quite fast and easy once you get the procedure down.

On-bike cleaning. For a new chain, prevent gunk from ever building up by cleaning the chain after wet or dirty rides. Use a snap-on cleaner, available from several companies. All have a reservoir for solvent and brushes that scrub the links as they pass through. Because you don't have to remove the chain, a cleaner is especially helpful for Shimano Hyperglide chains, which require a special new rivet for each re-assembly.

To use a snap-on cleaner, put newspapers below the drivetrain, put on your goggles and rubber gloves, fill the reservoir with solvent, snap it onto the chain, and backpedal until the links sparkle. Finish by wiping any excess off the chain, chainrings, cogs, rear derailleur, and frame. Let the chain dry, then put a drop of lube on each link juncture as you slowly backpedal. Continue turning the crankarm to help the lube work in, then wipe off the excess with a clean rag. Remember, you want lube inside the links, not on the outside where it will quickly attract more dirt, dust, sand, and so on.

Chain removal. Chain cleaners can't handle a sludge-encrusted chain. You need to remove it for soaking and scrubbing. Place the bike in a repair stand and shift to the smallest cog and chainring. Place the chain rivet extractor on a lower link and carefully begin to drive a rivet (use any silver one on Hyperglide models) by turning the tool's handle. If the rivet resists, unscrew the tool, check its alignment, and try again. Push the rivet until it's flush with the back of the tool (see photo on page 54). Don't push it out entirely unless you're working on a Hyperglide chain. Unscrew and remove the tool. Flex the chain laterally to separate the ends, then pull the chain from the bike.

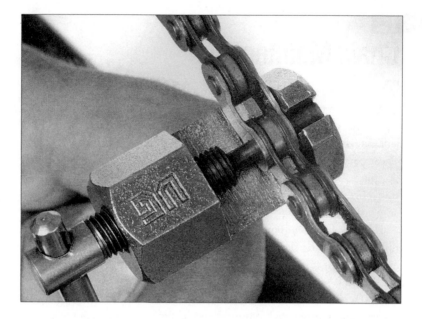

Cleaning in solvent. Work in a well-ventilated area and wear your
goggles and gloves. Pour an inch of solvent into a bucket, submerge the
coiled chain, and let it soak for a few minutes while you wipe down the
rest of the drivetrain with a solvent-dampened rag. Remove the rear
wheel, lightly spray the cogs with WD-40, than slip a rag between each
pair and buff them clean as if you were shining shoes. When done, don
goggles and gloves, hold the chain over the bucket, and brush it clean
link by link. Wipe it with a fresh rag and hang to dry. Some cyclists like
to rotate two chains so one is always clean and ready while they're
working on the other.

Measuring chain wear. Lay the chain on its side, stretched taut and
straight on the workbench. Put the first mark of a ruler on the center of
any rivet. The 12-inch mark should also align with the center of a rivet.
If the second rivet is more than ⅛ inch past the foot mark, the chain is
worn and should be replaced to prevent accelerated wear to the cogs
and chainrings. A new chain is likely to have more links than you need,
so match it to the old one and shorten it with the chain tool.

Installation. Before installing a freshly cleaned chain, lay it on a rag
and lubricate it thoroughly. Let it sit, then wipe off the excess. Feed the
end of the chain without a protruding rivet over the small chainring,

through the front derailleur cage, over the smallest cog, and through the derailleur pulleys. (If there is a protruding rivet on the chain's other end, it should be pointing toward you.) Then lift the chain off the chainring and rest it on the bottom bracket. For conventional chains, pull the two ends together so the protruding rivet snaps into place. Use the chain tool to drive the rivet home, ensuring that it protrudes an equal amount on both sides of the link. For Hyperglide chains, hold the two ends together, insert the tapered end of the Shimano special rivet, and drive it through until it clicks in place. Snap off the end with pliers or the end of the chain tool.

Freeing stiff links. Joining the chain usually causes a stiff link. Loosen it by gripping the chain with your thumbs on either side of the balky rivet. Flex the chain laterally. (Some chain tools have a provision for loosening stiff links by placing the chain on a second, higher flange and pushing the rivet through just slightly.) Double-check for stiffness by working the link up and down, then backpedal and watch the chain wind through the pulleys. A stiff link will jump a bit as it negotiates these tight bends.

Corrosion can freeze any link. Apply a penetrating lube such as WD-40 and use the flexing technique to loosen it. If this doesn't work, try pushing the rivet in slightly from one side, then back from the other. Flex the chain again. Still stuck? Replace the bad link.

After cleaning a chain or installing a new one, it's important to test ride the bike. New chains or even clean ones may skip on worn cogs, an annoying and dangerous condition where the chain lifts off the cog and

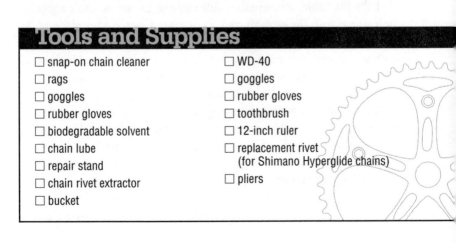

Tools and Supplies

- ☐ snap-on chain cleaner
- ☐ rags
- ☐ goggles
- ☐ rubber gloves
- ☐ biodegradable solvent
- ☐ chain lube
- ☐ repair stand
- ☐ chain rivet extractor
- ☐ bucket

- ☐ WD-40
- ☐ goggles
- ☐ rubber gloves
- ☐ toothbrush
- ☐ 12-inch ruler
- ☐ replacement rivet
  (for Shimano Hyperglide chains)
- ☐ pliers

jumps forward. Check for this by riding in each gear while gingerly standing on the pedals. Note which cogs skip (usually the smaller ones in combination with the small chainring) if you intend to replace cogs individually. Or you can replace the entire cassette, then maximize its life with regular chain maintenance.

14
Rear Derailleur Tune-Up

Whether your bike has index shifting (your lever clicks when you shift) or the almost extinct friction type, rear derailleur adjustment is the same except that an index shifter must be switched to friction mode during the procedure and then returned to index mode afterward.

Shift to the smallest cog. Place the bike in a repair stand so you can pedal by hand. Shift the chain to the smallest cassette cog and the middle or smallest chainring. Be certain that the rear shift lever is at the beginning of its range of motion, no matter what type of lever it is.

Place an index lever in friction mode. This isn't possible for all brands or models. Under-bar shifters, Shimano STI, Campagnolo Ergopower, and Grip Shift can't be switched from index. With other systems, you may be able to turn a D-ring or small lever. Look for instructions on the shifter body.

Lube the cable. Remove the cable end cap, loosen the cable anchor bolt, and extract the cable. If it's kinked, rusted, or frayed, replace it. Same goes for any cracked or corroded pieces of housing. Grease the sections of cable that run inside housing and reinstall the cable through the anchor bolt, but don't tighten it yet. Turn the derailleur's cable adjustment barrel clockwise all the way, then unscrew it one turn.

Check range of motion. While pedaling with your right hand, push the derailleur body with your left thumb, causing a shift to the largest cog. Release it to let the chain return to the smallest cog. Repeat several times, watching for any hesitation or overshifting.

Set the limit screws. If necessary, adjust the derailleur's range of motion by turning the high- and low-gear limit screws, which are usually the top and bottom screws, respectively (see photo). This will allow

the derailleur to shift precisely to the largest and smallest cogs. Counter-clockwise turns allow the derailleur to move farther. Clockwise turns reduce its range.

Test adjustments. With the chain on the smallest cog, use pliers to grasp the short section of cable that extends through the anchor bolt. Pull lightly to remove slack, then tighten the bolt. Install the cable end cap and crimp it in place with diagonal cutters. While pedaling with your left hand, shift the lever repeatedly with your right to test your derailleur adjustments. The chain should engage the largest and smallest cogs promptly and accurately. Adjust the limit screws as necessary. If the chain won't drop smartly to the smallest cog despite limit screw adjustments, the cable is probably too tight. Add slack by turning the adjustment barrel clockwise one-

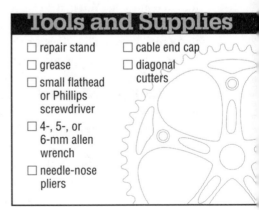

Tools and Supplies

- [ ] repair stand
- [ ] grease
- [ ] small flathead or Phillips screwdriver
- [ ] 4-, 5-, or 6-mm allen wrench
- [ ] needle-nose pliers
- [ ] cable end cap
- [ ] diagonal cutters

half turn. Otherwise, finish this step by removing any slack that's developed by opening the anchor bolt and gently pulling the cable through again (with the chain on the smallest cog).

Switch to index mode (if applicable). While pedaling with your left hand, move the shift lever one click with your right. The chain should jump to the second-smallest cog and run quietly. If it hesitates, screw the adjustment barrel counterclockwise one-half turn and try again. If it overshifts, screw the barrel clockwise by half-turns. Shift through all the cogs from each chainring to verify that the indexing is correct, then take a test ride. Fine-tune if necessary.

15
Front Derailleur Tune-Up

When your front derailleur is working well, shifts are seamless. The chain flows from one chainring to another without rattling, scraping, hesitating, or slipping. What's that? Your shifting sounds like a horse-drawn corn thrasher? Use the following steps to check and correct all the insufficiencies.

Check the bottom bracket. Put the bike in a repair stand. Check the tightness of each crankarm's fixing bolt, then grasp the crankarms and push and pull laterally to test for play in the bottom bracket. If you feel some in a traditional bottom bracket, use the lockring spanner and pin tool to remove it. (You may first need to remove the left crankarm by unscrewing its bolt and using a puller.) For a cartridge bottom bracket, make sure the retaining rings are tight. If movement persists, the cartridge may be defective. A loose bottom bracket causes the crankset to waver during pedaling, contributing to poor front shifts.

Straighten the chainrings. Like a loose bottom bracket, chainrings that move back and forth hinder shifting. Set the chain on the bottom bracket, then turn the crankarm by hand while looking at the chainrings from above. Using one side of the derailleur cage as a reference, observe the trueness of each ring. If they wobble in unison, the crankarm spider is probably bent. You may be able to straighten it with judicious raps from a plastic mallet (steel will damage the metal). Chainrings that wobble independently of each other can be trued with a small adjustable wrench. Open the jaws just enough to slip onto the big ring between two teeth, then gingerly bend wayward sections into alignment. It's hard to get at the smaller rings. Use the wrench or pry them with a large screwdriver. If all this makes you too nervous, have a shop mechanic do the truing. Also straighten or file any bent or damaged teeth.

Check the cable. Place the chain on the small ring. Remove the cable end cap, loosen the cable anchor bolt, and pull the cable from the housing (if applicable). Replace a rusted or frayed cable and cracked or corroded housing. Thread the new cable through the lever, housing or bottom bracket guide, stops, and anchor bolt. Don't tighten it yet. Apply spray lube to the derailleur pivot points and wipe off the excess. Check the tightness of all nuts and bolts.

Check alignment. When viewed from above, the outer side of the derailleur cage should be parallel to the chainrings. At least that's the place to start. A slight toe-in or toe-out may achieve even better shifting and chain clearance, but that's akin to splitting hairs. Next, look at the derailleur and rings from the side. Pull the cage outward with your hand. It should clear the large ring by $\frac{1}{16}$ inch. That's close. Rotate the crankarm to see if there is a high section in the chainring (often the case as teeth wear) and make your measurement there. If necessary, loosen the frame clamp with an allen wrench to adjust derailleur position.

Set the low-gear screw. Shift to the largest cassette cog and smallest chainring. Adjust the low-gear (inboard) limit screw so there is $\frac{1}{32}$-inch clearance between the inside of the inner cage plate and the chain (see

Tools and Supplies

- ☐ repair stand
- ☐ bottom bracket lockring spanner
- ☐ adjustable cup pin tool
- ☐ crankarm bolt wrench
- ☐ crankarm removal tool
- ☐ cartridge retainer-ring tool
- ☐ plastic mallet
- ☐ 6-inch adjustable wrench
- ☐ large flathead screwdriver
- ☐ small, flat file
- ☐ grease
- ☐ cable end cap
- ☐ diagonal cutters
- ☐ spray lube
- ☐ 8- and 9-mm combination wrenches
- ☐ 4-, 5-, and 6-mm allen wrenches
- ☐ small screwdriver
- ☐ pliers

photo). Clockwise turns close the distance to the chain; counterclockwise turns increase it.

Secure the cable. Make sure the front shift lever is fully in its starting position. Pull lightly on the cable end with pliers to remove slack, then tighten the anchor bolt.

Set the high-gear screw. Shift to the largest-ring/smallest-cog combination. Adjust the high-gear (outboard) limit screw so there is at least $1/32$-inch clearance between the inside of the outer cage plate and the chain. Make sure the cage doesn't move outward so far that it's touched by the crankarm. Clockwise turns reduce the cage's outward range; counterclockwise turns increase it.

Test adjustments. Shift the bike repeatedly in all chainring/cog combinations. Move the lever forcefully to stretch the cable and reveal any tendency to overshift. Stop with the lever in its starting position and the chain on the small ring, check for cable slack, and remove slack as in step 5. Go for a test ride. If overshifting occurs (the chain falls to the bottom bracket or off the outside of the big ring), tighten the appropriate limit screw one-half turn at a time and see if that's enough. If the chain hesitates in dropping to the small ring or climbing onto the big one, loosen the appropriate limit screw one-half turn at a time.

16

Replacing Derailleur Cables

Derailleur cables wear more quickly than brake cables because they're thinner and used more frequently. Due to this and the fact that a broken shift cable can leave you in a knee-straining gear, it's smart to check them monthly for rust and fraying (usually seen at the levers or bottom bracket guides). Also check housing sections for kinks or cracks, which can inhibit cable movement, fray the cables, or allow water to enter and cause corrosion. If you find any flaws in the system, eliminate them by replacing the problem cable and housing.

Cables and housing vary in design, length, and quality. For longevity, proper fit, and precise index shifting, buy replacements that match the original parts as closely as possible. The best way is to take the old items or your bike when you go shopping at the bike store.

Routine Service

Lubrication is the key to accurate shifts and long cable life. Many newer bikes have split cable stops that allow you to quickly lubricate without using tools. You should do this monthly and after a wet ride. Place the bike in a repair stand and shift to the largest chainring and second-largest cog. Return the levers to their starting positions without pedaling, creating cable slack. Pull the housings from the stops and slide them. Wipe and grease the newly exposed sections of cable, then hook things back up. But if you see any corrosion or damage, replace the parts using the following steps. Both cables are discussed below, but you needn't replace both if only one is going bad.

Remove old cables. With the bike in the repair stand, shift the chain onto the smallest chainring/cog combination. If the cables have end caps, remove them with cable cutters. Incorrectly attaching new cables will mess up index shifting, so be sure to note how the old ones fit into the derailleurs (sometimes they lie in a shallow groove). Then loosen the anchor bolts and slide the old cables from the housing and shift levers. Older-style Grip Shift shifters must be disassembled to remove the cables. Have a shop do the job. Don't try to pull frayed sections through housing or levers, because the wires may stab you and the cable can get stuck. Instead, cut off bad sections. Save everything for sizing the replacements.

Prepare new cables and housing. If the replacement cables have heads at each end, snip the ones that don't fit your levers. Grease the sections that will be inside the housing. If you're also replacing housing, use diagonal or cable cutters to trim the new pieces to size. Inspect the housing ends to ensure that you haven't created a burr that will cause drag and fray the new cable. To remedy a burr, trim it with diagonal cutters then smooth it with a file. If the original housing has metal or plastic ends (ferrules), install them on the new sections, too, and lightly grease the tips.

Installation. The chain must be on the smallest cog and chainring, and the shift levers must be in their starting positions. (Push the return lever on systems such as Campagnolo Ergopower, Shimano STI, and Shimano Rapidfire until they stop clicking.) Also, turn all cable adjustment barrels clockwise until they stop, then back them off one turn. These barrels may be located atop the rear derailleur, at the down-tube cable stops, or on mountain bike shift levers.

Now you're ready to thread the cables. Be sure the heads are seated in the levers and that housing ends are seated in their stops. Pass each cable through its anchor bolt, grab the end with pliers, and pull it firmly (but not so hard that you move the derailleur). Tighten the anchor bolt (see photo). Cut off all but an inch of excess cable, slide on an end cap to prevent fraying, and crimp it in place.

Stretch the cables. Spin the crankarm and shift repeatedly to test and stretch the new cables. Leave the chain in the small chainring/cog combo, then check each cable for slack by twanging a bare section. If there is slack, loosen the anchor bolt and pull the cable taut with pliers.

Adjust derailleurs. If necessary, correct shifting problems using the

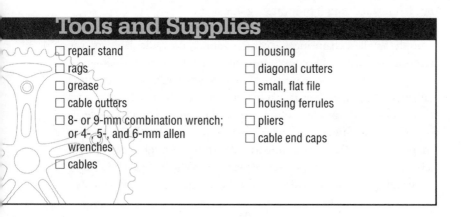

Tools and Supplies

- ☐ repair stand
- ☐ rags
- ☐ grease
- ☐ cable cutters
- ☐ 8- or 9-mm combination wrench; or 4-, 5-, and 6-mm allen wrenches
- ☐ cables
- ☐ housing
- ☐ diagonal cutters
- ☐ small, flat file
- ☐ housing ferrules
- ☐ pliers
- ☐ cable end caps

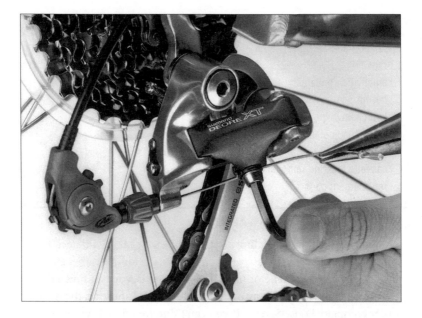

advice in chapters 14 and 15. Accurate index shifting requires precise cable tension. If the rear derailleur hesitates on shifts to larger cogs, tighten the cable by turning an adjustment barrel counterclockwise in half-turn increments, checking performance each time. For slow shifts to smaller cogs, make clockwise half-turn adjustments. It's easy to remember this when using the barrel located where the cable enters the derailleur. Just turn it in the direction the derailleur hesitates, for example, toward the larger cogs for slow shifts when the chain climbs onto them, or toward the smaller cogs when the chain balks at dropping down.

17
Replacing Cogs

After installing a new chain, you may also need to replace one or more cogs to prevent skipping—the disconcerting and sometimes dangerous tendency of the chain to lift off the teeth and jump forward. Worn or broken teeth can cause this problem on individual cogs, while a stiff chain link usually skips on every cog.

Tools and Supplies

- [ ] repair stand
- [ ] rags
- [ ] small stick-on labels
- [ ] felt-tip pen
- [ ] two chainwhips
- [ ] 12-inch adjustable wrench
- [ ] grease
- [ ] cassette lockring remover
- [ ] replacement cogs

- [ ] freewheel remover
- [ ] freewheel vise
- [ ] bench vise
- [ ] spray or drip lube

Find worn cogs by pedaling forcefully in each gear. If you need to re-place three or fewer, it's cheaper to buy cogs individually rather than purchasing a new cassette or freewheel—if, that is, you can find a shop that stocks single cogs. Many no longer do. A good source is the mail-order company Loose Screws. If you can't find individual cogs or most are worn, replace the entire unit.

Just so you're clear about the terminology, a freewheel is what is found on older bikes. It contains the ratcheting mechanism and screws onto a threaded hub. Most newer bikes have a cassette that slides onto a splined, ratcheting hub body.

Determine your system. To proceed with cog replacement, you first need to determine which type, brand, and model of cog cluster you have. Place the bike in the repair stand, open the brake quick-release, shift to the small chainring/cog combo, open the hub quick-release, and remove the wheel. Unscrew the quick-release nut and pull out the skewer. Look for the brand and model name on the cogs or on the face of the lockring around the axle. Freewheels have notches or splines on this face to accept a tool for unscrewing it from the hub. Most newer cassettes such as Shimano Hyperglide and Campagnolo models are held to the hub by splined lockrings that also require removers. Older cas-settes have no visible splines or notches and are disassembled using two chainwhips.

Mark the cogs. Before disassembly, clean the cogs by sliding a rag be-tween each pair. Mark their front sides and orientation with small stick-on labels and a felt-tip pen. Later, during disassembly, label the spacers as well. These steps aren't crucial on most cassettes, which have identical spacers and cogs that can be installed just one way. But it's very helpful on freewheels, where spacers and cogs vary.

Unscrew the first cog. For freewheels and older Shimano cassettes (as well as some rare brands), lean the wheel against your legs, cogs facing out. Wrap the chain of one whip clockwise around the largest cog so that the handle is on your left, parallel to the floor. Wrap the second whip counterclockwise around the smallest cog so its handle is on your right, parallel to the floor. Bend over, grasp a handle in each hand, and push down on both to break the smallest cog loose (see photo).

Exchange cogs. With a cassette, you can slide off the remaining cogs once the smallest is unscrewed. Some Shimano cassettes connect the cogs with long, thin bolts that you'll have to unscrew before you can replace any cogs. With a freewheel, repeat the chain whip procedure on the other threaded cogs until you reach the splined ones. Lift them off the freewheel body. Now replace the bad cog(s) and reassemble the freewheel after lightly greasing all threads.

Remove cassettes with lockrings. To remove a Shimano Hyperglide or Campagnolo cassette, start by positioning the wheel as you did to unscrew the first cog. Wrap the chain of one whip clockwise around

the largest cog until the handle is on your left, parallel to the floor. Place the appropriate remover into the lockring. While holding the whip handle, turn the remover counterclockwise with an adjustable wrench to unscrew it. Remove the lockring and washer (if any). Slide the remaining cogs off the cassette body. There are cassette models such as the Shimano Dura-Ace on which you'll find several cogs attached to a holder. If you have this type, the cogs must be replaced as a unit. Replace the offending cogs and slide everything back onto the body. Lightly grease the lockring threads, then snug it with the remover tool and adjustable wrench.

Balky Freewheels

Freewheel cogs may be so tight that they cannot be disassembled on the wheel. If this applies, follow this step and the next. First, remove the freewheel from the hub. Start by clamping the appropriate remover in place with the quick-release skewer (leaving off the conical springs). Hopefully, this will prevent the remover from slipping. Lean the wheel against your legs, cogs facing away. Position a large adjustable wrench on the remover so you can press down on it with your right hand, turning it counterclockwise. Once the freewheel starts unscrewing, remove the skewer and continue turning the remover with your fingers.

Mount the freewheel in a freewheel vise. Clamp it in a bench vise. Now you can disassemble the freewheel by unscrewing the smaller cogs with a chain whip and lifting off the splined ones. Label everything or carefully lay parts down in order so you don't mix up the spacers and forget which direction the cogs face. Replace the bad cogs. Grease all threads lightly before reinstallation. Tighten the threaded cogs with the chain whip. Flip the freewheel over and lube its bearings through the crack between the outer and inner body. Let the lube soak in. Then grease the threads and carefully screw it onto the hub. Snug it by turning it clockwise with a chain whip.

PART FIVE

Internal Bearings

18

Bottom Bracket Overhaul

A conventional bottom bracket should be disassembled and repacked once a year—or anytime the bike suffers through an excessively wet or dusty period that could contaminate the grease. You can easily identify this type of bottom bracket by looking at the left side of the frame down at the crankarm axle. There will be a slotted lockring around a separate adjustable cup. If instead you see a splined, recessed retainer ring, the bike has a cartridge bottom bracket, and you should turn to chapter 19.

Remove the dustcaps. Put the bike in the repair stand. Set the chain on the bottom bracket. Spray WD-40 through the crankarm dustcap holes, wait a minute, then unscrew the dustcaps. The type with two small holes requires a special pronged pin tool (snap-ring pliers may work). Plastic caps with a slot at the edge can he pried off with a small screwdriver. Other types accept a large flathead screwdriver or 5-mm allen wrench. Remove frozen dustcaps by tapping counterclockwise on one hole or the edge of the slot with a screwdriver and hammer. For frozen allen-wrench–type dustcaps, drill two holes and use a pin tool.

Remove the crankarms. Unscrew the crankarm bolts or nuts with a socket wrench. Be sure to remove any washers. Back out the crankarm removal tool's plunger, then firmly screw this tool into an arm. When you're sure the tool is seated completely, turn the plunger clockwise with a socket wrench to extract the arm. Repeat for the other arm.

Disassemble the bottom bracket. Remove the bottom bracket lockring from the bike's left side by turning it counterclockwise with the lockring wrench. Remove the adjustable bottom bracket cup (on the same side) with the pin tool. Pull out the axle and the bearings. Now go to the other side of the bike and check that cup with a fixed cup wrench. If it's tight, there's no need to remove it. Otherwise, take it out. (*Note:* On most bikes, the fixed cup is reverse threaded. It unscrews by turning clockwise.)

Clean the parts. Make sure everything is out of the bottom bracket, including the protective plastic sleeve (if so equipped). Put all parts in solvent. Don goggles and gloves, then brush all parts clean. If you didn't

Tools and Supplies

- ☐ repair stand
- ☐ WD-40
- ☐ adjustable pin tool
- ☐ socket wrench
- ☐ large flathead screwdriver
- ☐ hammer
- ☐ crankarm removal tool
- ☐ bottom bracket lockring wrench
- ☐ bottom bracket fixed cup wrench
- ☐ biodegradable solvent

- ☐ bucket
- ☐ goggles
- ☐ rubber gloves
- ☐ brush
- ☐ rags
- ☐ flashlight
- ☐ grease
- ☐ ¼-inch ball bearings (22) or bearing retainers
- ☐ thread adhesive

remove the fixed cup, reach through the frame with a rag and wipe it clean. If reusing bearing retainers, carefully pop out the bearings with your fingers. (Don't bend a metal retainer.) Clean both retainers thoroughly. If you scrub the crankarms, keep solvent away from the pedals.

Inspect for damage. Dry all parts with a rag. Inspect the cups and axle for pitting or scoring (cavities or roughness on the bearing tracks). If you didn't remove the fixed cup, use a flashlight to check it. Replace anything that's damaged with parts of identical dimensions.

Lubricate. Grease the retainers and pop in new ball bearings. Place a medium layer of grease in both cups and install the retainers, making sure they aren't upside down. If you're uncertain, hold a cup in one hand and insert the axle. It should contact the balls, not the retainer. The axle should spin smoothly with no drag. After the retainers are in their cups, cover them with a thin layer of grease. If the crankset has loose balls instead of retainers, set the balls in the grease you've put in each cup. Almost all cranksets use 11 balls in each side. Also put a little grease on the shoulders of the axle where the bearings roll.

Install. Wipe the threads inside the bottom bracket. Start screwing in the fixed cup (if removed) and apply two drops of thread adhesive to the threads. Install the fixed cup as far as possible and tighten it as firmly as you can with the fixed cup wrench. To prevent rust on a steel frame, lightly grease the center of the bottom bracket shell. Apply grease to the center of the bottom bracket axle and insert it. Be very careful not to dislodge loose balls. The long end of the axle goes toward the drive-train. (Any letters or numbers in the middle of the axle would appear right side up if you were to look at them from astride the bike and could see through the frame.) Install the plastic sleeve (if used) and adjustable cup with bearings.

Adjust. Use the pin tool to screw the adjustable cup into the frame while wiggling and turning the axle by hand to feel for play. When there's none but the axle spins freely, thread on the lockring and tighten it gently. Wipe off the axle tapers and bolt on the right crankarm. Push and pull it laterally to feel for play in the bottom bracket adjustment. Use the lockring wrench and pin tool together to fine-tune the cup adjustment (see photo). When it's right, lock it in place by holding the cup still as you tighten the lockring securely. Install the left crankarm. Grease both crankarm bolts, then tighten them very firmly. Install the dustcaps after greasing their threads (if applic-able).

After a couple of rides, check all adjustments. Remove any lateral play by tightening the adjustable cup, and make sure the crankarm bolts are snug.

19

Cartridge Crankset Service

While crankarms and chainrings haven't changed drastically in the last decade, bottom brackets have. Bikes made since the 1992 model year probably have a Shimano cartridge-style sealed bottom bracket. (Most other bikes have a traditional cup-and-cone bottom bracket that can be disassembled and regreased as described in chapter 18.)

Cartridges are durable, are easy to install, and require little maintenance. The disadvantage is that they aren't rebuildable. They must be replaced if they fail. Here's how to inspect and service your cartridge crankset and how to install a new unit when the inevitable day arrives.

Tighten the crankarm bolts. Do this monthly, before an important event, or if you hear creaking or clicking from the crankset. Most bolts these days are allen bolts, which are easily accessed. Others may have dust-caps. If yours do, pry off or unscrew them, tighten the fixing bolts with a crankarm bolt wrench or standard socket wrench, and replace the caps. Then check the tightness of the chainring bolts by turning each one clockwise with a 5-mm allen wrench. On a triple crankset, the bolts that attach the smallest chainring are on the inside, facing the bottom bracket.

Straighten the chainrings. If the chain rubs the front derailleur cage during a portion of each pedal stroke, or if you experience skipping or unwanted shifts up front, your chainrings may be damaged. To check them, shift to the small ring and place the chain on the frame's bottom bracket shell. Turn the crankarm and view the rings from above, using the cage as a reference. Look for wavers or bent teeth.

If the large ring wobbles away from the frame, strike its outside face at the correct spot with a plastic mallet. Hit it fairly softly at first, spinning the crankset between blows to check your progress. If the wobble is to the inside or if one of the smaller rings is bent, place the broad blade of a long screwdriver against the bad spot and rap the end of its handle with a hammer. Again, proceed cautiously so you don't cause a waver in the opposite direction.

Realign bent teeth with an adjustable wrench. Slip the jaws over each one and gently pry it into alignment. Use a file to smooth any burrs or hooks.

Inspect the bottom bracket. A sealed-cartridge bottom bracket is designed to be maintenance-free. It should last at least two years before the lubricant dries, then it should be replaced. Once each month, tighten the crankarm bolts, then check the cartridge's condition by grasping the crankarms (not the pedals) and pushing and pulling laterally. There shouldn't be any play. If there is, the retention rings may not be holding the cartridge securely or the cartridge could be worn. A loose retention ring is also indicated by clunking or creaking during pedaling.

Check the cartridge axle. If you detect a problem, you need to determine exactly what is causing it. Set the chain on the bottom bracket shell. Remove the crankarms by unscrewing the bolts (take out the washers, if any) and using the crankarm removal tool made for your crankset.

Check the cartridge's condition by turning the axle with your fingers. It should spin smoothly with slight resistance caused by the grease inside. Replace the cartridge if the axle feels very rough when you turn it or if it spins without resistance (a sign that the grease is gone).

Tighten the cartridge. If the axle seems fine, tighten the cartridge. This requires a cartridge retainer ring tool such as the Park BBT-2 that fits into the retention rings (you must have the correct tool for your model of bottom bracket cartridge). Place the tool into the right-side

Tools and Supplies

- ☐ repair stand
- ☐ 5-, 6-, 7-, and 8-mm allen wrenches
- ☐ crankarm bolt wrench
- ☐ large flathead screwdriver
- ☐ plastic mallet
- ☐ hammer
- ☐ medium adjustable wrench
- ☐ small, flat file
- ☐ ⅜-inch–drive ratchet

- ☐ crankarm removal tools (depending on your model, these could include an allen wrench, dustcap remover, socket wrench, and puller)
- ☐ cartridge retainer ring tool appropriate for your bottom bracket model
- ☐ cartridge crankset
- ☐ grease
- ☐ rags

ring. Remember, this side of the bottom bracket has reverse threads, so turn the tool counterclockwise with a ⅜-inch–drive ratchet or adjustable wrench until it's snug. Then turn the left ring clockwise until it's very tight. Reinstall the crankarms, dustcaps, and chain.

Cartridge Removal

If turning the axle tells you there's a problem inside the cartridge, install a new unit. To remove the old cartridge, use the cartridge retainer-ring tool to completely unscrew the left retention ring (counterclockwise). Then place the tool in the right side and turn it clockwise until you can extract the cartridge (see photo). To obtain an exact replacement, use the identifying number on the unit or take it to a shop.

Cartridge Replacement

To install the new cartridge, grease the threads lightly and insert it from the right side. Engage the threads by turning it counterclockwise a couple of revolutions. Screw the left-side retainer ring clockwise until it's about halfway in. Go back to the right ring and turn it until it's snug against the frame. Finish by firmly tightening the left ring. Install the crankarms and chain, and you're ready to roll.

20

Hub Overhaul

Your bike will have one of three types of hubs: traditional ball and cone, labyrinth-sealed ball and cone, or sealed cartridge. The first two are easy to service; the last can be relatively easy or next to impossible for do-it-yourselfers, depending on its design. Consult your owner's manual or a local bike shop for advice.

Don't base your servicing schedule on mileage or time. Rather, remove the wheels from your bike monthly (twice a month for mountain bikes ridden off-road) and spin the hub axle between your thumb and forefinger. Assuming the cones are properly adjusted, the axles should turn smoothly. If there is grinding or binding, or if they turn too freely, the grease has probably washed out or dried up. In either case, it's time to overhaul the hub.

The following instructions are for rear hubs because they are more complicated. Except for removing and reinstalling the cassette or free-wheel, front-hub overhaul is identical. (Some rear hubs require cassette removal, others don't. A freewheel always needs to come off.)

Prepare your work space. Spread a clean rag to catch ball bearings or, even better, work over a cafeteria tray. Pour an inch of solvent into a wide-mouth jar. A solvent that's labeled "biodegradable" is relatively safe and effective, but make sure there is plenty of ventilation and wear your goggles. Have several clean rags within easy reach. Unwrap and segregate the new ball bearings in separate jar lids. Most front hubs take 10 of the $\frac{3}{16}$-inch balls per side, although some use 9 of the $\frac{7}{32}$-inch balls. Almost all rear hubs use 9 of the $\frac{1}{4}$-inch balls per side. You could clean and reuse the old bearings but that's false economy. New bearings are inexpensive and guard against premature wear to other internal parts.

Disassemble the hub. Take the wheels off the bike, remove the quick-release skewers or axle nuts, then wipe the grime from the axles so you can see what you're doing. Remove the cassette or freewheel from the rear hub (see chapter 17 for instructions). Place the rear wheel on your work area with its left side up. With the appropriate cone wrenches, unscrew the locknut and slide off all washers. (On some hubs you may have to remove a rubber or plastic dustcover to see the axle parts.) Then unscrew the cone, allowing the axle to drop out the underside.

Tools and Supplies

- ☐ rags
- ☐ biodegradable solvent
- ☐ jar and lids
- ☐ goggles
- ☐ correct-size replacement bearings
- ☐ chainwhips
- ☐ large adjustable wrench
- ☐ freewheel or cassette remover
- ☐ metric ruler

- ☐ cone wrenches
- ☐ large flathead screwdriver
- ☐ rubber gloves
- ☐ toothbrush
- ☐ cones
- ☐ grease
- ☐ plastic mallet

Some bearings will probably remain in the hub while others cling to the greasy axle or cones. Discard them as you find them unless you need to measure them for getting replacements. Put all of the other parts in the solvent.

Clean. Remove the dustcap on the hub's left side by gently levering it upward with a large flathead screwdriver. (If the dustcap is difficult to remove, leave it in place—it makes cleaning more difficult but not a lot, and you'll avoid damaging the dustcap.) Put the cap in the solvent if you removed it. Flip the wheel and repeat this step for the right side. Wipe out the hub shell, including the center. If necessary, dip the corner of a rag in solvent, but be sure to wipe away all traces when done. Put on rubber gloves, fish each part from the solvent, and scrub it with a toothbrush. Wipe each part with a clean rag and lay it to dry.

Inspect the cones and races. Each cone will have a shiny ring where the bearings roll. Look closely for any pits in this polished path. Replace both cones if even one has this defect. An unevenly worn path or a crack in the cone are also grounds for replacement. These problems will eventually deform the bearings, which in turn will deform the races in the hub shell, forcing you to replace the hub (replaceable races are extremely rare)—quite an expense compared to the price of cones. Inspect the hub-shell races for excessive wear, using the same criteria as with the cones. If the races are damaged, you'll probably have to replace the hub as races can rarely be replaced. Next, check the axle for straightness. To facilitate reassembly, first measure the exact position of the right-side cone. Then remove the cone, washer(s), and locknut. Roll the axle on a hard, flat surface. A slight deformity is not unusual in a rear axle. Anything greater means it's bent and should be replaced.

Lubricate the hub. Wash your hands. Spread a thin layer of grease around one hub race. Lay in the new bearings, then put another layer of grease over them (see photo), smoothing it with your finger. Insert the dustcap if it was removed and tap it in place with a mallet, if necessary. Gingerly turn the wheel over and repeat these steps for the other side. The dustcap and grease should hold the first side's bearings in place.

Install the axle. Screw the right-side cone, washer(s), and locknut onto the axle, stopping the cone at the correct distance. Firmly tighten this assembly by using the cone wrenches to screw the cone and locknut toward each other. Coat the face of the cone with a thin layer of grease. Insert the axle through the right side of the hub. Apply grease to the face of the left cone and screw it on until it's finger tight. Install the washer(s) and locknut, tightening it against the cone with the cone wrenches.

Adjust the cones. Check cone adjustment by alternately turning the axle and rocking it sideways. You have it right when the axle spins smoothly and feels just a smidgen loose. This allows for the cones to be compressed inward when the wheel is tightened in the frame. If you still

feel play when you move the installed wheel from side to side, snug the cones a bit. If the weight of the valve stem (positioned at three or nine o'clock) isn't enough to turn the wheel, the cones need to be backed off a bit. Often, this is as easy as putting a cone wrench on each side and simultaneously screwing the cones apart (left hand pushing forward, right hand pulling back). If they give a little, it usually does the trick. Keep fussing until you get it right.

21
Cassette Care

During the 1990s, freewheels gave way to cassettes on most good bikes. Among the advantages are simplified cog replacement, either individually or as a unit. Unscrew the lockring, then the rest slide right off. Also, on most cassettes, the cogs have ramps and specially shaped teeth to help the chain climb up to larger sizes or drop down to smaller ones. All in all, cassettes are a big improvement.

Maintenance is pretty simple, too. Unlike with a freewheel, a cassette's ratcheting mechanism and bearings are part of the hub. As this procedure explains, you don't have to disassemble anything tricky to pack this cog holder's 50 bearings with fresh lube to ensure optimum performance and longevity. The job is made even easier with a neat tool called the Freehub Buddy (about $25). It works for the various Shimano cassettes found on many road and mountain bikes. The first time to service your cassette is when you buy a new bike, because factory lube is minimal. After that, service the holder each time you clean and lube the hub.

Remove the cogs. Take off the rear wheel, then unscrew and extract the quick-release skewer. Spritz the cogs with WD-40 to loosen the grime. After a minute, slide a rag back and forth between each pair to clean them. Next, lean the wheel against your shins with the cassette facing out. To remove it, place a chain whip on a middle cog with the handle pointing left. Put the cassette lockring remover in place, gripping it with a large adjustable wrench pointing right. Hold the chain whip to prevent the cassette from rotating, and push down on the adjustable wrench to unscrew the lockring. Then lift off the cogs. Place all parts on a rag in the order of removal.

Remove the axle. Working on the left side of the wheel, remove the hub's conical rubber seal (if there is one), place a cone wrench on the cone, and unscrew the locknut by turning it counterclockwise with another cone wrench. Slide off the spacer, unscrew the cone, and extract the axle plus all of the ball bearings from each side (usually, there are 9 per side). Place all parts on the rag.

Inspect the hub. There's a dustcap on the hub's right side. Gently (some force is required) pry it out with a flathead screwdriver. Then clean the cones, bearings, and hub by wiping them with a rag. Use solvent if necessary, and remember to wear your goggles and gloves. Inspect all parts for excessive wear or pitting, and replace anything that's going bad. If the hub's bearing races show damage (pits and cracks) you should replace the hub or buy a new wheel.

Clean the cassette holder. Turn the holder with your fingers. If it feels smooth and clicks smartly, follow the directions for lubing it that appear on page 79. If it feels crunchy, you must clean it. Apply a little grease to the Freehub Buddy's O-rings and press it into the holder. Fill an oil can or baster with a solvent that's compatible with the lube you plan to use for the hub bearings. (Use synthetic with synthetic, petroleum-based with petroleum-based.) Lay the wheel on rags atop your workbench, with the Freehub Buddy facing up. Put the tip of the oil can or baster into the fitting/hole. While slowly rotating the holder, pump in

Tools and Supplies

- ☐ WD-40
- ☐ rags
- ☐ chain whip
- ☐ cassette lockring remover
- ☐ large adjustable wrench
- ☐ cone wrenches
- ☐ medium flathead screwdriver
- ☐ biodegradable solvent
- ☐ goggles
- ☐ rubber gloves
- ☐ grease
- ☐ Freehub Buddy
- ☐ oil can or turkey baster
- ☐ solvent that's compatible with oil or grease for bearings
- ☐ oil or grease
- ☐ small needle-type grease gun
- ☐ ball bearings

solvent until it seeps out the back by the hub flange (see photo). Dirt enters primarily from the back side, so this treatment flushes it out in that direction. Keep at it until the cassette holder spins smoothly.

If your cassette is not by Shimano or if you don't have a Freehub Buddy, you can clean the cassette holder by squirting solvent into the opening between the inner and outer bodies of the holder. Rotate the outer body (the inner body will remain stationary) while applying solvent so that it works its way into the internal parts of the body.

Lube the cassette holder. Use a thick oil (for temperatures below 40°F) or a thin grease. For oil, fill the can (after removing any solvent), press the nozzle into the Buddy, and pump until oil flows out the back. For grease, fill the grease gun, place the nozzle in the Buddy, and pump until you see it oozing out the back. (If you don't have a Buddy, lube the cassette holder with the same technique that you used to clean it.) Wipe away the excess. You'll notice that the holder spins more quietly now.

Reassemble the hub. Pack grease in both cups and insert new ball bearings in each side. Press in the right-side dustcap, making sure it's fully seated. Use cone wrenches to be certain the axle's right-side cone and locknut are tight against each other, then insert the axle through the hub. Put on the left-side cone, spacer, and locknut. Using two cone

wrenches, adjust the left side until there's only a smidgen of lateral play when you wiggle the axle. (This will disappear when you clamp the wheel in the frame.) Then lock the adjustment by tightening the cone and locknut against each other.

Install the cogs. Slide the cogs onto the holder and thread on the lockring, tightening it clockwise with an adjustable wrench. Insert the quick-release and put the wheel back in your bike. Be sure that it is centered and that it spins freely without hitting the brake pads.

22
Conventional-Headset Overhaul

It's easy to forget about the headset if it's working properly. But this important part of your bike should be overhauled once each year, more often if it's subjected to heavy use, rough ground, mud, dust, or water. A neglected headset will be quick to wear its cups and cones, necessitating complete replacement.

The headset components work together to hold the fork in the frame while permitting it to rotate freely for steering. Rattling, clunking, grinding, or a notchy or stiff feel are all symptoms of an overdue headset overhaul.

A conventional headset is used with a fork that has a traditional threaded steerer tube extending up through the frame's head tube. During the 1990s, a revolutionary threadless design gained popularity, particularly on mountain bikes. If that's the type of headset you have, turn to chapter 23.

Clear the way. Put the bike in the repair stand and remove the front wheel. It's easier to do this work if the front brake is disconnected (cantilever or parallel-pull) or removed (sidepull). You don't need to unbolt the latter's cable. Just unscrew the attaching nut behind the fork crown, remove the brake, install the nut and any washers so you don't lose them, then place the brake out of the way by securing it to the handlebar with tape or a rubber band.

Wrap tape around the stem to mark its height in the headset. Unscrew the stem's expander bolt (directly above the headset) with four

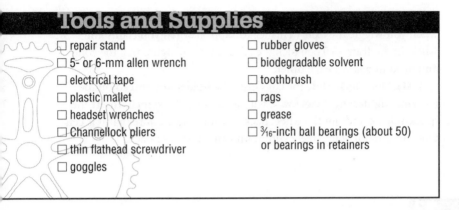

Tools and Supplies

- ☐ repair stand
- ☐ 5- or 6-mm allen wrench
- ☐ electrical tape
- ☐ plastic mallet
- ☐ headset wrenches
- ☐ Channellock pliers
- ☐ thin flathead screwdriver
- ☐ goggles

- ☐ rubber gloves
- ☐ biodegradable solvent
- ☐ toothbrush
- ☐ rags
- ☐ grease
- ☐ ³⁄₁₆-inch ball bearings (about 50) or bearings in retainers

counterclockwise turns. Strike the bolt with a mallet, or lay a piece of wood on it and hit that with a hammer. This frees the plug that secures the stem inside the fork's steerer tube. For sunken bolts, leave the allen wrench in place and strike that. Remove the handlebar/stem and hook it over the top tube.

Disassemble. Unscrew the top nut by using one headset wrench on it and the other on the flats of the adjustable cup just below it. Turn the top nut counterclockwise. If it won't budge, reinstall the front wheel and hold it between your legs for more leverage. Remove all but the adjustable cup and place the parts in sequence on your workbench so you'll remember their order. If a notched lockwasher is stuck, grip it with your Channellock pliers and align its peg or flat with its counterpart on the steerer tube. Use a thin screwdriver to pry off a tight washer.

Unscrew the adjustable cup as you hold the fork in the frame with your other hand. Soon you'll see a retainer full of ball bearings. Note that the open side of the retainer's "C" shape faces down. Slide the fork out of the frame, exposing the lower bearing retainer. Keep the two sets of bearings separate in case they're not identical in size and number (but they usually are).

Clean and inspect. Don your goggles and gloves, then soak and brush each removed part with solvent. Use a rag to wipe grease from the parts still in the frame and on the fork. Then inspect everything for excess or uneven wear, pits, dents, and cracks. If you determine that the headset is shot, take the bike to a shop to have a new one installed. The required tools are too expensive unless you'll be servicing several bikes for a few years. If everything is in good shape, proceed to the next step.

Lubrication. Wipe the steerer tube with a rag, then coat its entire length with a thin film of grease. This prevents corrosion. Put an even layer of grease into the cup at the bottom of the head tube and on the race at its top as well as in the adjustable cup. If your replacement bearings are loose rather than in retainers, carefully dislodge the old balls, clean and dry the old retainers, then press in new balls (see photo). Don't forget the orientation of the retainers in the headset as you're handling them. Pack the retainers with grease.

Reassemble the headset. Place the bearing retainer on the fork race, then slide the fork into the frame. Place the bearings on the upper race. Thread the adjustable cup down the steerer tube until it contacts the bearings, then back off one-eighth turn. Replace all of the other parts in order, but don't tighten the top nut. Turn the stem's expander bolt just enough for the plug or wedge to make contact, then grease the stem as far up as the tape. Install the bar/stem to its correct height and tighten.

Adjust. Tighten the top nut. Check for correct adjustment by levering back and forth with one hand on the fork and the other hand holding the handlebar, feeling for headset looseness. Next, turn the bar fully to the left and right to feel for binding. Correct for any play or tightness by loosening the top nut and moving the adjustable cup. It'll

probably take a few tries to get it just right. It's better to work from too loose, because overtightening can damage the headset. Once the adjustment feels correct, lock it by tightening the top parts toward each other (top nut clockwise, adjustable cup counterclockwise).

Reattach the brake and front wheel. Loosen the stem bolt, align the stem with the wheel, then snug the bolt. Not too tight—it must be tight enough not to turn when you hit a bad bump but you want the stem to pivot in the steerer tube during a crash to reduce the chance of parts breakage and personal injury.

Tip: The most common problem with headsets is called brinnelling. This is the term for distinct dents around the upper and lower bearing paths. The dents cause a rough notchy feel as the handlebar is turned. If you're experiencing this problem and your bearings are in retainers, you can usually revive the headset by rebuilding it with loose balls. This trick works because at least one extra bearing fits in each race, so the balls no longer align with the dents. It's tedious but not impossible to get loose balls to stay in place as the headset is reassembled. Use extra grease to hold them better.

23
Threadless-Headset Overhaul

Dia-Compe's AheadSet was a truly revolutionary product when it was introduced in the early 1990s. First seen on mountain bikes, AheadSets and the competitors that have been spawned now grace even some top-end road machines. This clever design saves weight, uses a more robust threadless fork-steerer tube, and is easier to service than a conventional headset.

Here's how it differs: On a conventional threaded headset, the cone and top nut are tightened against each other to lock the adjustment. Unfortunately, hard riding can loosen the parts, and this leads to damage. With a threadless headset, the parts simply slide onto the steerer tube and the stem's pinch bolt(s) locks the adjustment. It does this so well that, ordinarily, no amount of hard riding will loosen it.

There are several AheadSet models and similar threadless versions made by other companies. Most common is the AheadSet Kontak from Dia-Compe or Cane Creek, so that's the one that is used for the following instructions. Higher-priced bikes may have a model with sealed-cartridge bearings, which are designed to be maintenance-free. That version of the AheadSet is called S Series.

A Kontak-series AheadSet, like any serviceable headset, should be overhauled at least once each year (every six months if you frequently ride in wet or dusty conditions). Here's how to clean and inspect the parts and install new bearings and grease.

Check the condition. Listen for a clunk when you lift the front of the bike several inches and drop it. Or put the bike in a repair stand, remove the front wheel, grasp the handlebar in one hand and the fork in the other, and lever back and forth. Any headset looseness will be apparent. Then check for binding by turning the handlebar slowly and fully in each direction. It should rotate with no tight spots. If the headset is loose, a simple adjustment may suffice. (Go to step 6.) If it's rough or binding, dirt may have penetrated the seals, so an overhaul is needed.

Disconnect the front brake. With the bike in the repair stand and the wheel removed, disconnect the cable from the lever of a cantilever or parallel-pull brake. For sidepulls, remove the brake by unscrewing it from the back of the fork crown. Put the nut and any spacers back on the bolt for safekeeping. Hang the brake on the handlebar end and secure it with a rubber band or tape.

Disassemble the headset. Unscrew and remove the allen bolt on top of the stem, and extract the top cap. (As you proceed, place all parts on the workbench in order of removal.) Wrap a rag around the frame's top tube. Loosen the pinch bolt(s) that secure the stem, then hold the fork and lift off the handlebar/stem. Rest it on the top tube and secure it with a rubber band. Pull the spacers off the top of the steerer tube. If you have a rigid fork, you may have to remove a cable hanger. Pull down on the fork or tap the top with a plastic mallet

Tools and Supplies

- ☐ repair stand
- ☐ rubber bands
- ☐ 5- and 6-mm allen wrenches
- ☐ rags
- ☐ plastic mallet
- ☐ goggles
- ☐ rubber gloves
- ☐ biodegradable solvent
- ☐ toothbrush
- ☐ 5/32-inch loose bearings (44) or bearings in retainers
- ☐ grease

AheadSet Kontak headset

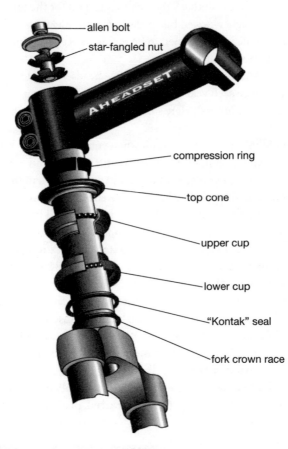

allen bolt

star-fangled nut

compression ring

top cone

upper cup

lower cup

"Kontak" seal

fork crown race

to free the compression ring and top cone, then lift them off. Next re-move the top bearing retainer. (Be sure to note its orientation in the cup.) Now extract the fork from the frame and place it on your work-bench.

Clean and inspect. Slide the lower bearing retainer off the fork crown race. (If it's not there, it's still inside the lower frame cup.) Don your goggles and gloves, and use solvent to clean all the parts that have been removed or are still in the frame. As you wipe them dry, inspect for damage. The cups, cone, and crown race should be smooth where the bearings contact them. If they're pitted, dented, rusted, or cracked, have a shop mechanic replace the headset. (Special tools are required to press-fit the parts.) Otherwise, pop out the old balls, being careful not to bend the retainers. Scrub the retainers with a toothbrush, dry them completely, then insert new bearings.

Lube and reassemble. Start reassembly by lightly greasing the steerer to prevent corrosion, but stop short of the top section that the stem clamps to. Put an even layer of grease in both cups. Pack the retainers with grease and place them in the cups. Make sure the retainers are oriented correctly. Reinstall the fork and slide the upper parts onto the steerer tube. Install the stem (but don't tighten) and top cap. Apply a little grease to the top allen bolt and screw it into the threaded insert (called a star-fangled nut) that's inside the fork steerer tube. Or, if you have an aftermarket multi-piece top cap that cinches inside the steerer, seat it and snug the allen bolt to lock the base of the mechanism in the fork.

Adjust. Be sure the stem bolt(s) are loose. Snug the top allen bolt just enough to remove play without introducing any tightness. Keep in mind that this is not the bolt that holds the stem onto the steerer, so it doesn't require excessive torque. In fact, some top caps are designed to break if the bolt is tightened too much. (If moderate tightening doesn't remove play, consult shop personnel.) Turn the fork slowly and push and pull it to check the adjustment. When it's right, align the stem and tighten its bolt(s) to lock it. Tighten the cable hanger (if applicable). Reattach the brake cable or caliper. Install the front wheel, check the brake adjustment, and have a nice ride.

24
Pedal Overhaul

Road bike pedals require minimal maintenance. They stay pretty clean and aren't frequently exposed to conditions that can contaminate their internal parts. But off road, it's a different story. Pedals are dirt magnets. Ignore them, and troubles soon begin.

This discussion is about clipless pedals for two reasons. First, they have overwhelmed the road and mountain bike markets, relegating traditional pedals with toeclips and straps to inexpensive, low-performance bikes. Second, their cleat-engaging mechanism is exposed and susceptible to becoming fouled. This can cause big problems when

Tools and Supplies

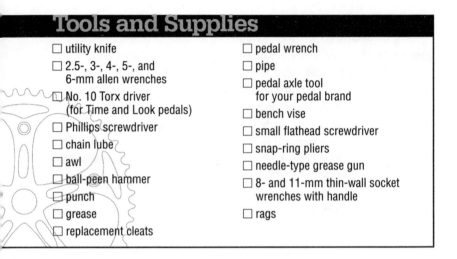

- ☐ utility knife
- ☐ 2.5-, 3-, 4-, 5-, and 6-mm allen wrenches
- ☐ No. 10 Torx driver (for Time and Look pedals)
- ☐ Phillips screwdriver
- ☐ chain lube
- ☐ awl
- ☐ ball-peen hammer
- ☐ punch
- ☐ grease
- ☐ replacement cleats

- ☐ pedal wrench
- ☐ pipe
- ☐ pedal axle tool for your pedal brand
- ☐ bench vise
- ☐ small flathead screwdriver
- ☐ snap-ring pliers
- ☐ needle-type grease gun
- ☐ 8- and 11-mm thin-wall socket wrenches with handle
- ☐ rags

trying to click in or out, especially in an emergency. Untended long enough, clipless pedals may also develop loose parts or bad bearings. Because pedals usually cost a fair bit, it makes sense to keep them working well for as long as possible.

Note to users of traditional pedals: These are usually inexpensive. If something goes wrong internally, it's probably not worth the time and trouble to fix it. Instead, buy a new pair or upgrade to clipless. But if you do want to try an overhaul, you'll find the same internal axle/bearing/cone/washer/locknut system as in conventional bottom brackets, headsets, and hubs. Remove the pedal dustcap, then follow the principles for disassembly, cleaning, inspection, lubing, and rebuilding.

Okay, here's how to service a clipless pedal system.

Adjust tension. If you're having trouble getting in or out of a new pair of clipless mountain bike pedals, make sure the recessed cleat engages the pedal properly. With certain shoe/pedal combinations, the soles may hinder engagement. Trim the hole around the cleat with a sharp utility knife to increase clearance. Still not working well? Most pedals have a spring-tension adjustment. Look for a small allen screw on the front and back of double-sided off-road pedals or on the rear of single-sided road pedals. Turn the screw counterclockwise to ease cleat entry and release. Lightly lube the cleat and mechanism. While you're at it, check the snugness of all other screws.

Replace the cleats. Trouble releasing from pedals usually means the cleats are worn. Replace them before the problem becomes persistent.

First, mark the position of the old cleats by scratching their outlines on the soles with an awl. If the cleat bolts won't loosen, use a hammer and punch to drive them counterclockwise. Install new bolts with greased threads to prevent removal problems in the future. Then align and tighten the new cleats.

Remove the pedals. The remaining steps are best done with the pedals off the crankarms. Shift to the large chainring and set the crankarms horizontal, right pedal forward. Attach a pedal wrench to either pedal so it's just above the crankarm, then push down to loosen and unscrew. (The left pedal unscrews clockwise.) If either pedal won't budge, slip a pipe over the wrench handle for extra leverage.

Check the bearings. After the pedals are off, spin the axles between your fingers. Do they turn with no resistance at all? Do they feel dry, loose, or rough? If so, you need to service the bearings. But if the axles turn smoothly without looseness and you feel a slight hydraulic resistance, the grease and adjustment are still fine. Grease the threads, reinstall the pedals, and you're done.

Open the pedals. To take apart most clipless pedals (including Look, VP, and some Shimano), unscrew and remove the axle and bearings as a unit (see photo). Check for a splined plastic or aluminum ring, or wrench flats. Unscrew the axle/bearing assembly with a pedal axle tool,

Channellock pliers (on aluminum pedals only), or a wrench. With the right pedal held in a vise with the axle upright, turn the tool clockwise to unscrew the axle; turn the left pedal counterclockwise.

Follow the procedure for your brand. For a Shimano 535 pedal, use a small screwdriver to pry out the plastic dustcap on the end, exposing the bearings. For a Ritchey Logic pedal, unscrew the dustcap with an allen wrench, then unscrew the 8-mm nut beneath it and remove the axle. It's unlikely you'll need to disassemble Time ATAC or Speedplay Frog pedals, because the bearings are well-sealed. But if you're convinced they need service, here's how. On ATACs, look for a recessed snap ring where the axle enters the pedal body. Remove it to extract the axle and access the bearings. To disassemble a Frog, unscrew the two allen bolts holding the body together as well as the tiny bolts on its end.

Regrease. If you add grease every few months, the pedals may never need new parts. For Shimano 747 and 737, Look S2 and SL3, and similar pedals with cartridge axle/bearings, put a tablespoon of grease inside the pedal body and reinstall the axle assembly (don't force it; screw it in a bit and remove it, and repeat until it seats). This automatically regreases all the bearings. Lube Speedplay Frogs by removing the tiny allen bolts in the end and pumping in grease with a needle-type grease gun. For Shimano 535 pedals, push grease into the exposed bearings and the inside bearings (after retracting the rubber seal). Grease the bushings in Ritchey pedals after axle removal.

Rebuild. New internal parts are required only if the pedals are shot. To do this work you may need special tools. Some manufacturers such as Ritchey offer rebuild kits that include instructions. For Look pedals, you'll need new axle assemblies. Disassemble one pedal at a time so you can use the other one to figure out how to put the first one back together. Clean everything, inspect the parts, replace those that are worn or damaged, regrease, and reassemble.

PART SIX

Mountain Bike Particulars

25

General Tune-Up

At midseason, it's tune-up time if you've been riding your mountain bike regularly. By attending to a few details, you'll keep your scoot humming till the snow flies. Chances are good that it doesn't need major work, especially if it's decent quality and not too old. You should easily be able to do the work yourself using the following steps. If you find a problem that's not covered here, turn to the appropriate chapter and make that repair as well.

Clean and inspect. Working outside, wash the bike with a sponge and warm, soapy water. (Don't do the drivetrain yet.) Rinse well, then dry with rags. As you do, inspect the frame tubes, fork, pedals, tires, grips, saddle, cables, housings, brake pads, and so on and list any problems. Cracks in the paint may mean cracked or bent tubes, which should be evaluated by bike shop personnel. Tires with cuts or decaying sidewalls should be replaced, as should frayed cables, damaged housing, ripped grips, and worn brake pads. Most pads have vertical grooves. When these disappear or the material is less than 3 or 4 mm thick, new pads are in order.

Measure the chain. Start your ruler on the center of any pin and see if the 12-inch mark is on the center of another pin. If the mark is more than ⅛-inch short of a pin, the chain has stretched to the point where it needs to be replaced. (You may need new cogs, too.) While working with the chain, sight down its length as you turn it slowly so you can spot bent links. If there are any, replace the chain.

Check the chainrings. Have you been suffering from chainsuck? This frustrating problem occurs on shifts to the small chainring. The chain hangs on the teeth and is pulled upward by the next pedal stoke, jamming between the chainring and stay. This scars the frame and can bend the chain links or chainring. Chainsuck is usually caused by a sludgy, sticky chain or worn, hooked teeth that don't release the chain under hard pedaling pressure. Assuming the chain is okay, the small ring is probably faulty and should be replaced. The other chainrings should run true and not have any damaged teeth. If you find some that are bent, gently pry them straight again with the jaws of a small adjustable wrench. Eliminate any burrs with a small, flat file.

Tools and Supplies

- ☐ sponge
- ☐ bucket
- ☐ detergent
- ☐ rags
- ☐ 12-inch ruler
- ☐ 6-inch adjustable wrench
- ☐ small, flat file
- ☐ repair stand
- ☐ spoke wrench
- ☐ tire pump with gauge
- ☐ shock pump
- ☐ 4-, 5-, 6-, and 8-mm allen wrenches

- ☐ crankset wrenches
- ☐ 10-mm combination wrench
- ☐ pedal wrench
- ☐ snap-on chain cleaner
- ☐ toothbrush
- ☐ biodegradable solvent
- ☐ goggles
- ☐ rubber gloves
- ☐ chain lube
- ☐ pliers
- ☐ spray lube
- ☐ Teflon lube

True the wheels. Put the bike in a repair stand. Make sure the wheels are centered and tight in the frame and fork. Check the hubs by wiggling the wheels laterally. If there's play, the hubs should be adjusted or even overhauled if it's been a year or more since they've been serviced. Next, check spoke tension. Start at the valve stem and work around the wheel, wiggling each spoke to find any loose ones. The left-side rear spokes will feel the loosest, but that's okay as long as they're similarly tensioned among themselves. If you find random loose spokes, tighten them with a spoke wrench until they match their same-side neighbors. You can tell by squeezing or plucking them. Spin the wheel, watch the gap between the brake pads and rim, and true the wheel using the instructions in chapter 7.

Pressurize. Proper tire inflation prevents pinch flats and rim damage. Make sure air pressure is in the range listed on the tire sidewall. If you have an air/oil suspension fork check its pressure, too. Adjust as necessary. Some forks have Schrader valves, which allow inflation and pressure readings with a regular pump and gauge. Others require a ball needle or special pump, which may have come with your bike. Check the bike manual or contact a shop or the manufacturer for recommended fork pressure.

Tighten up. Components may loosen with use, so it's smart to check them regularly. Work from stem to stern so you don't overlook anything. Tighten the following bolts by turning them clockwise with the correct wrench: (*Note:* If a bolt won't turn with moderate force, it's tight enough. Don't overdo it.) stem and handlebar binder bolts; suspension fork bolts; brake and shift-lever clamp bolts (reposition the parts first, if necessary); seat clamp and seatpost binder bolts; chainring and crankarm bolts (tighten these firmly); front and rear derailleur attachment and cable-anchor bolts; rear suspension pivot bolts; and accessory mounting bolts. Also tighten the pedals, remembering that the left one has reverse threads (meaning it tightens counterclockwise).

Service the drivetrain. There are two ways to clean the chain while it's on the bike. Either use a snap-on cleaner that has a solvent reservoir and rotating brushes, or scrub the chain with a toothbrush dipped in solvent. The former is quicker and usually more thorough. Remember to wear your goggles and gloves when handling solvent. When finished, wipe the chain well with a clean rag. While it finishes drying, remove the rear wheel and clean the cogs by sliding a rag back and forth between each pair. Clean the derailleurs and chainrings by wiping them with a solvent-dampened rag. Reinstall the wheel and lubricate the chain, wiping off any excess lube.

Tune the shifting. Have gear changes become sluggish when going to bigger cogs? If so, the cable has stretched a bit. To remedy this, place the bike in a repair stand so you can shift to check adjustments. Look for the knurled barrel at the back of the derailleur, where the cable enters. Turn it counterclockwise one-half turn and shift gears to judge performance. Continue as necessary until the chain climbs immediately onto the next bigger cog and still returns without hesitation to smaller ones. Listen for a rattling noise after each shift is completed. This means the chain isn't properly aligned with the cog it's on—it's probably touching the next bigger one. Turn the adjustment barrel clockwise to let out just enough cable to stop the noise.

Replace the brake pads. Remove and replace one pad at a time so you can use the opposite pad to gauge post location and angle. For optimum performance, new pads must strike the rim squarely but with a slight toe-in that causes the forward end to contact the rim first. This prevents squealing. After both pads are installed, squeeze the brake lever and watch to make sure the pads aren't partially above or below the rim. When they're right, grip each holder with an allen wrench or each pad with pliers so it can't change position, then firmly tighten.

Adjust the brake cables. Even if the pads aren't worn enough to warrant replacement, you may still have lost some stopping power. This happens because the levers must travel farther before the pads strike the rims. Tune the brakes by turning each brake lever's adjustment barrel counterclockwise until pad clearance is right, then run the lockring against the lever.

Lubricate. Finish by putting a shot of spray lube on the hinge or pivot of each brake, brake lever, derailleur, shift lever, and clipless pedal. Use a rag to stop overspray, and wipe off excess. Also lube each point where cables enter or exit housing or contact cable guides. For suspension forks, lift the boots, wipe dirt off the inner legs, apply a few drops of Teflon lube to the legs, compress the fork several times, and reattach the boots.

26
Suspension Forks

A suspension fork needs periodic maintenance and perhaps an occasional adjustment to continue working correctly. That's easy to say. Much more difficult is telling you how to do this work yourself. There are so many fork brands, models, and designs on the market that no uniform procedure can begin to cover them. Furthermore, suspension is still evolving. New front (and rear) shocks are being introduced every year as older versions become obsolete. The good news is that suspension designers are moving closer to parts that need infrequent (or no) major service.

To work on your fork, it's essential to obtain an owner's manual and follow its instructions. It will tell you the service intervals, procedures, and special tools you need. If a fork manual didn't come with your bike, check at a shop that carries your brand. Or, contact the fork's manufacturer by phone or on the Internet. Some Web sites have detailed repair and tuning advice. Be prepared with your fork's model name and identification number so you get the correct information.

All that said, there are some simple service guidelines and troubleshooting procedures that apply to most forks. These will help you care for the fork externally, but they don't go into its inner workings. Perhaps this is as much as you care to do as a home mechanic. If so, you can take the bike to the shop for fork repairs and overhauls as they're needed. It's still good to have an owner's manual so you can understand how your fork works and talk intelligently with shop personnel about its needs.

Adjust the range of travel. Suspension forks move a set amount, commonly 2 to 4 inches, between their resting and fully compressed positions. A fork should also sag a bit as you sit on the bike. This sag distance (preload) is specified by the manufacturer. To check it, fasten a zip-tie at the top of a fork leg. Sit on the bike to compress the fork with your body weight, then see how far the zip-tie has moved. Adjust preload until you get this distance right. Then go for a ride with the zip-tie still in place. Purposely hit some big bumps, hard. Afterward, you can determine the fork's travel based on the zip-tie's position. You want the fork to reach its maximum travel on the very biggest bumps to ensure that it's not adjusted too tightly, preventing it from fully absorbing smaller impacts.

Customize preload. Forks come from the factory adjusted for the weight of an average rider. But if you're relatively light or heavy, the fork may barely react to bumps or it may frequently bottom out with a harsh thunk. Should preload adjustments not be sufficient to correct this problem, consult a shop mechanic. Different internal parts may need to be installed.

Check the bolts. They must stay tight to ensure proper performance and prevent excessive wear. However, be very careful not to overtighten and strip threads or twist off a bolt head. It's best to follow the torque specifications in the owner's manual. If a bolt continually loosens, remove it and apply a liquid thread lock.

Observe the oil. If your fork has oil damping, a trace of external oil is common and nothing to worry about. If it's actually dripping, however, you probably have a blown seal or O-ring. The fork needs to be disassembled and repaired right away.

Bounce the bushings. The bushings between the fork's sliding and stationary legs wear with use or abuse. Check for the resulting play by squeezing the front brake and rocking the bike back and forth. If you feel looseness or hear knocking, it could be either bad bushings or a defective headset. If the headset is okay, the bushings probably need to be replaced. In most cases, this should be done by a pro mechanic with the appropriate tools.

Verify your lube. Don't just grab anything that's handy when lubricating your fork. Check the manufacturer's recommendation. The wrong product could harm internal plastic or rubber parts or cause a bad reaction with the lube already in the system.

Keep sliders slippery. Once a week, lift each fork leg's boot (if your bike has them), wipe off any dirt with a rag, and apply a little lubrication. Compress the fork to work the lube past the seals, then replace the boots. This lets the fork slide with as little friction as possible.

Replace bad boots. If the rubber boots on the fork legs become torn or quit sealing well for any other reason, replace them. You may see pro racers riding without boots in order to reduce friction and weight a bit, but they have team mechanics to rebuild the forks after every event. For the rest of us, boots are an effective defense against dirt and moisture. Of course, when washing your bike after a muddy ride, avoid spraying water at the boots or any fork seals.

Position the bumpers. On forks with double crowns, make sure the bumpers on the upper legs prevent metal contact with the frame when the fork pivots fully. The bumpers have to be placed precisely.

Beware of salty conditions. A seaside environment or the salt used to de-ice roads in winter can corrode the magnesium or aluminum used in most forks. If your bike is exposed to salty liquids, wash and dry it frequently, if not after every ride. Waxing the fork and other metal parts can help prevent damage.

Perform a postcrash inspection. You dump it hard during a ride and suddenly the fork doesn't work quite the same. In most cases, replacing the bad part or correcting misalignment will restore the fork to top performance. It's best not to ride the bike again until you've diagnosed the problem and, in most cases, fixed it. A fork that fails on the trail can cause a long walk home, or worse, a serious injury.

27
Rear Suspension

As with suspension forks, there are so many rear-suspension designs and frequent innovations that it's futile to discuss specific repair and maintenance procedures. In general, keep the suspension free of grimy buildup, regularly check bolts and pivots for looseness, and watch for oil leaks or marked changes in performance that say something is out of whack. Get the owner's manual for your particular equipment and follow its service and repair recommendations.

Several general principles apply to virtually every rear-suspension design. Tuning, which is the process of matching a rear suspension to your particular weight and terrain, lets you maximize bike handling, comfort, and overall off-road performance, but too many riders never bother to change the factory settings. It's an easy procedure, so here's how to do it.

First, some basics. There are two predominant types of rear suspension, or shocks: those with steel coil springs, and those with air springs. Nearly all are oil-damped. Damping controls the movement of the spring. Without it, your bike would bounce up and down on the trail like a pogo stick.

Another key term is "sag." This refers to how much the shock compresses under your weight. It may seem counterintuitive, but it's best to have some sag in your shock at all times. In fact, some experts call it the most important factor in suspension setup. Take away sag, and the rear wheel won't drop into a hole or track smoothly through chattery bumps. Your bike will buck like an ornery bull. Steps 1 through 5 deal with this important adjustment.

Measure stroke and calculate sag. "Stroke" (or the more common term, "travel") is the total distance your shock can move. Determining travel on coil shocks is a no-brainer. Simply measure the length of the shaft you see inside the spring (including the small rubber bottom-out bumper). On an air shock, part of the shaft is hidden, so you need to determine travel by checking the owner's manual or asking the bike dealer or manufacturer.

After you've determined travel, you can calculate the all-important sag. When you have your full weight on the bike, a shock should compress 25 percent. Therefore, multiply travel by 0.25. For example, a shock with 1.5 inches of travel should sag 0.38 inch when you're on board.

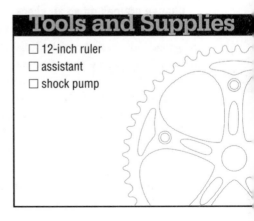

Tools and Supplies

☐ 12-inch ruler
☐ assistant
☐ shock pump

Measure total shock length. This is the distance from the center of one fixing bolt to the other. Take the measurement with no weight on the bike. Most commonly, you'll come up with a figure around 6.5 inches.

Measure existing sag. For this, you need a helper. Sit on the bike, supporting yourself with one hand on the wall. Put one hand on the handlebar, and clip your feet into the pedals. (To ensure an accurate weight, wear everything you do when riding.) Make sure any damping adjustments on your shock are in the middle of the range. Now have your friend measure the shock length. Subtract this figure from the unloaded total shock length.

Say you have a 6.5-inch-long shock. When you sit on the bike, it measures 5.7 inches. Your sag is the difference, or 0.8 inch. But hold on: The sag you actually want (step 1) is 0.38 inch. If the sag you measure is greater than what's recommended, you need to add preload. This makes the spring stiffer so it doesn't sag as much. If your sag is less than what it should be, you need to decrease preload (making the spring springier). To change preload, follow one of the next two steps.

Change preload on a coil shock. To increase, turn the knurled ring on the spring clockwise when looking down on the shock. To decrease, turn counterclockwise. Now recheck sag as in step 3. Keep adjusting till you get it right. *Note:* You shouldn't need to add more than four or five turns of preload. Never use pliers to force it. Conversely, you shouldn't have to turn the ring out so far that the spring loses tension. If either of these conditions exists, the spring isn't right for your weight and you should replace it with either a stiffer or more compliant one. Talk to your dealer or call the manufacturer for a replacement.

Change preload on an air shock. To do this, you need a special shock pump (about $30). Screw the pump fitting onto the shock's valve until the gauge indicates a pressure. Inflate to increase preload. To decrease preload, simply screw the pump on and off again, allowing a bit of air to escape. Recheck sag as in step 3, and readjust as necessary.

Adjust damping. Higher-price shocks have external damping adjustments. On the high-end Fox and Rock Shox systems, for example, there are two knobs—red for rebound, blue for compression. Start with both knobs in the middle of the range and take a ride. If the shock returns too quickly, causing the saddle to smack you in the butt, you have too little rebound damping. Turn the knob clockwise a click or two and try again. Conversely, too much rebound damping causes the shock to "pack up" when you hit a series of bumps, compressing more each time without returning, until all travel is gone. In this case, the shock isn't coming back quickly enough, so you need to decrease damping. Another rebound test is to push down on the seat. If it comes back very slowly, decrease damping.

Compression damping is available only on the most expensive shocks because most riders don't need it. It's used to reduce bobbing and give a more efficient ride on a long climb. Some shocks even supply a handlebar-mounted adjuster, enabling you to change compression on the fly. However, if your shock frequently bottoms out (reaches the end of its stroke with a thunk), don't compensate by cranking up the compression damping. It's better to correct this problem by altering preload or changing springs.

PART SEVEN

Detailing

28

Replacing
Handlebar Tape and Grips

Installing new handlebar tape or grips is the poor cyclist's paint job, quickly spiffing up the appearance of your trusty rig. There's a practical reason to replace these parts, too. Worn tape or grips don't supply a secure handhold, which could result in a slip and loss of steering control. Here's how to handle these simple jobs.

Replacing Tape

Remove the old tape. It's easier to work if the bike is in a repair stand. Usually, tape is wrapped from the end of the bar to the center, which creates a shingling effect that prevents the overlaps from being separated by hand pressure. If so, there will be a band of adhesive-backed finishing tape on each side near the stem. Unwrap it. Sometimes tape is installed from the center, in which case the loose ends are tucked under the end plugs. Carefully pry out the plugs with a flat screwdriver. (Some plugs have a screw in the center. Loosen this several turns, then tap it in before prying out the plug.)

Clean the handlebar. Most newer bikes have housing for the brake or shift cables under the tape. If you have bar-end shifters, note how much of each side's shift-cable housing is covered by the tape, so you can match it when retaping. Then unwind the old tape from the bar. Non-adhesive plastic will come right off. Adhesive types can tear and leave residue, so work slowly to limit this problem. Then use alcohol to loosen and remove the remnants.

Prepare the brake levers. If short strips of tape aren't supplied in the package of handlebar tape, cut a 4-inch-long piece from the end of each roll. Turn back the brake lever hoods and apply these pieces horizontally to cover the bands that hold the levers on the bar.

Begin taping. Go to either end and start the new tape beneath the bar. Stand in front of the bike with the wheel steadied against your knee. Gently stretch the tape as you wind it on, removing wrinkles and keeping it tight. Overlap by about one-third of the tape width, enough for the adhesive strip (if any) to contact the bar. Be careful not to leave gaps underneath as you go around the curve and up to the brake lever. If the bar is grooved for cable housings, hold the housings in place with strips of electrical or duct tape.

Wrap the levers. When you reach a brake lever (the hood should still be rolled back), use a figure-eight pattern. After the last wrap to the base of the lever, bring the tape diagonally up behind the lever and then across the top. Go down on the opposite diagonal, around the bottom again, then back up (see photo). Keep the tape taut through all this to prevent wrinkles. There should be no gaps revealing bare metal, thanks to the short tape pieces on the brake lever bands. Then continue wrapping until you approach the center of the bar. There may be a decal, engraving, bulge, or lip that delineates where to finish wrapping. Repeat on the other side, then roll the hoods back into place.

Secure the ends. If the center of the bar does not have a distinct shoulder, finish winding so that a straight edge results. On a bulged bar, the tape edges should be flush with the larger-diameter section. Cut the tape so its end is beneath the bar, then secure it with a double wrap of electrical tape. (Instead of plain black, consider a hue that matches your frame's color or use thin strips in multiple colors for a custom look.) Slightly stretch the electrical tape so it lies flat. For a pro look, don't overlap the finishing tape sideways—a single width is correct. Trim it so the end is hidden below the bar.

If the bar has a sharp lip at the center, wrap over it, pulling tightly. Then unwrap the tape and look for a diagonal impression. Cut along

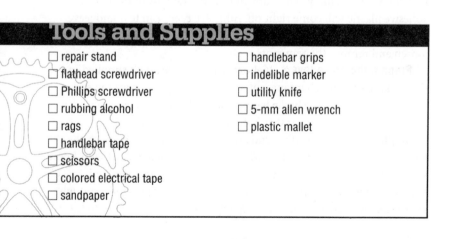

Tools and Supplies

- [ ] repair stand
- [ ] flathead screwdriver
- [ ] Phillips screwdriver
- [ ] rubbing alcohol
- [ ] rags
- [ ] handlebar tape
- [ ] scissors
- [ ] colored electrical tape
- [ ] sandpaper

- [ ] handlebar grips
- [ ] indelible marker
- [ ] utility knife
- [ ] 5-mm allen wrench
- [ ] plastic mallet

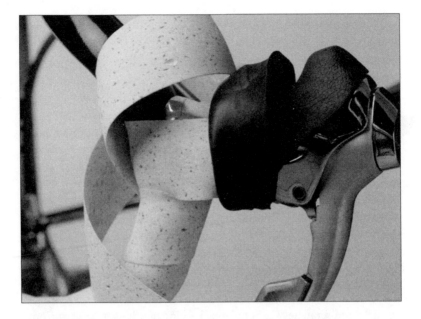

this mark with scissors. When you rewrap, the end of the tape will fit perfectly against the lip and the finishing tape will fit flush.

Install end plugs. If yours have screws, turn them clockwise to tighten. Sometimes end plugs fit loosely and could fall out. If so, wrap them once or twice with electrical tape before pressing them in. If plastic plugs have sharp edges, sand them smooth. Never ride without plugs. The open end of a bar can cut you badly if it strikes you in a crash.

Replacing Grips

Remove end caps and bar-ends. Pry out each handlebar end cap (if any) with a flat screwdriver. If you have bar-ends, use a marker to make reference lines on them and the bar so you can reinstall them in the same position. Then remove them using a 5-mm allen wrench.

Remove the grips. Slit the old grips lengthwise with a utility knife (don't scratch the bar), then peel them off.

Dribble a little alcohol into each new grip. This helps them slide onto the bar, then it quickly dries so the grips won't slip.

Cut off the ends of grips. If the grips have closed ends and you're using bar-ends, tap the grips with a mallet. Like a cookie cutter, the handlebar will neatly sever the ends.

Reinstall bar-ends and end caps. Slide the grips inward until there's enough room for the bar-ends, then install them in line with your reference marks and tighten securely. Tap in the end caps.

29
Frame Paint Touch-Up

There are two absolutes about frame touch-up, according to frame-builder and restorer Peter Weigle. First, you absolutely must cover bare metal spots on a steel frame to protect its integrity. Second, the repair absolutely won't look as good as new. Still, it's much better than allowing a bike to suffer ugly and dangerous rust. Even for painted noncorrosive frame materials such as aluminum (which can corrode when subjected to excessive salt), titanium, and carbon composite, touching up nicks and scratches keeps the bike looking new longer (at least from a few feet away). Otherwise, those who own a nonsteel frame are spared from most of the following preventive and restorative chores.

Here are the frame care procedures that Weigle and other pros recommend.

Match the paint. This is difficult because even original paint will appear lighter or darker when brushed on rather than sprayed. It's even tougher if you can't get the stock color. (You can check with a bike shop or the bike's manufacturer but it's unlikely they'll have the correct paint unless you're touching up a bike from the current model year.) A solution is to peruse the model-paint section at a neighborhood hobby store and purchase the closest color you can find. If it's not close enough, try mixing colors. Nail polish is another excellent touch-up paint substitute, and it comes in a myriad of hues.

Fill a fresh nick. Clean the area to be painted with rubbing alcohol and allow it to dry for 10 minutes. Position the bike with the nick facing up. Use a tiny paintbrush, a toothpick, or the fuzzy end of a cardboard match to carefully apply paint to the flaw. Avoid getting it up on the edges of the nick. If necessary, repeat this step until the nick is evenly filled with paint. Don't apply additional paint before the drying interval specified on the label. Let the paint cure for two weeks. (You can ride the bike in the meantime.) Then clean the spot, apply a fine rubbing compound, and buff it with a soft cloth. Finish the job with a dab of frame wax.

Cover a large chip. Large chips and scratches require more work. Start by feathering the edges by wet-sanding with 600-grit paper. Don't remove any more paint than necessary to get a smooth edge. Clean the area with alcohol. Paint the chip with a brush that's sized for the job. Continue to wet-sand and apply more paint at the specified intervals until you achieve the desired result. After two weeks of curing, rub and wax the spot.

Repair rust. Remove rusty spots by carefully sanding or scrubbing with a tiny wire brush. Problem areas include top-tube cable guides, pump fittings, the area under the rear brake cable, and nooks around the lugs, fork crown, and bottom bracket. When all traces of corrosion are gone, clean the bare metal with alcohol, then cover each spot with a rust-inhibiting primer such as Rust-Oleum. Paint over it with your touch-up color, or don't bother if you'll be having your frame professionally stripped and repainted at the end of the season.

Camouflage. If your attempt at repair looks as bad as the original flaw, you can cover it with a sticker, decal, or colored plastic tape. The key on a steel frame is to paint the nick or prime the rusty spot before covering it, so corrosion won't start underneath.

Provide impact protection. Wrap several layers of colored electrical tape around the top and down tubes at the spot where the front brake or handlebar could swing around and cause a chip or dent (match the

Tools and Supplies

- ☐ touch-up paint
- ☐ rubbing alcohol
- ☐ rags
- ☐ assortment of small paintbrushes
- ☐ rubbing compound
- ☐ frame wax
- ☐ 600-grit sandpaper
- ☐ small wire brush
- ☐ rustproof primer
- ☐ decals and stickers
- ☐ colored electrical tape
- ☐ Weigle Frame Saver
- ☐ spray polish
- ☐ toothbrush
- ☐ chrome polish
- ☐ Simichrome

frame color and the tape will almost disappear). If the right chainstay is getting hammered by the chain, cover the stay with a strip of tape or a commercial slap panel.

Work on internal defense. Weigle began undercoating the insides of his frames with an industrial anticorrosion compound. When he realized how effective this was at protecting the steel from insidious internal rust, he began marketing the substance as Weigle Frame Saver in a handy spray can. The product is available at bike shops. It's never too late to start using it. A good time is when you have the bike stripped of components for a major overhaul.

Take preventive measures. Protect the outside of your frame by waxing it twice a year and applying a spray polish every week or two. Keep your eye on the potential rust trouble spots mentioned above. When applying wax, use a soft toothbrush to work it into tight or detailed areas such as around lugs, cable guides, the bottom bracket, and the fork crown. Sweat tends to pool in these areas and accelerate corrosion. Keep chrome clean and waxed from day one because there's no hope once it begins to pit. Simichrome helps restore the luster to aluminum alloy.

PART EIGHT

Special Service

30
Breaking In a New Bike

I bought a lemon!" This is a fear many bike buyers develop a few weeks after wheeling their sparkling new machine out of the store. Almost every dealer can tell tales of customers angrily returning their bikes, complaining of loose crankarms, wobbly wheels, and derailleurs that don't shift accurately anymore. But these aren't fatal flaws or even something to worry about. They're merely part of breaking in a new bike. This is why most shops offer a free tune-up 30 days after purchase. Take advantage of it, then use the procedures in this book to take care of future service.

Why tune-up after 30 days? Because within this time the cables on a new bike can stretch enough to hamper braking and hinder shifting. The spokes will fully seat, causing the once perfectly true wheels to wobble. The bolts that attach the crankarms and other parts may loosen. Internal bearings settle in and may allow play. Once readjusted after this break-in period, all of these parts should be fine for a long time.

However, if you pass up this free service and keep riding despite the niggling problems, they'll only become worse. Ignore loosening crankarms, for instance, and the excess wear at the place where they attach to the bottom bracket axle can make it impossible to ever keep them tight. A crankarm could even fall off while you're riding, causing a crash or at least a lot of inconvenience.

Here's a rundown of the problems a new bike can develop during the initial few rides. Because the shop will do the 30-day tune-up for free and expertly, have them solve the following problems.

Floppy cables. If the brake levers begin reaching the handlebar before you get good stopping power and the bike no longer shifts as well as during the first few rides, everything is perfectly normal. New cables stretch, and the remedy is as simple as opening the anchor bolts and removing the slack. Even though you can do this yourself, it's good to let the shop handle it in case something else may be faulty with the brakes or derailleurs. Also, removing slack from a rear derailleur cable may necessitate a slight gear adjustment. For a quick, no-tools, temporary remedy, turn the adjustment barrels on the brake levers or calipers and on the back of the rear derailleur counterclockwise to tune the adjustments.

Loose bearings. Bearings in the bottom bracket, headset, and hubs are properly adjusted when they're free of side play but turn smoothly. The catch is that bearings can be perfectly adjusted when installed, yet settle in enough to develop play after a few miles. To detect this, wiggle your wheels sideways, rock your bike back and forth with the front brake applied, and try to move the crankset sideways by levering with the crankarms. A loose bottom bracket can also result from cups that weren't tightened properly when installed. Side play may damage the internal parts and should be corrected as soon as you notice it.

Stiff chain link. A mechanic who installs a chain will make sure the joining link bends smoothly. But sometimes a chain comes from the factory with a tight link somewhere else. If your feet occasionally skip forward slightly when pedaling, suspect this problem. To check, get off and hand shift into the smallest chainring/cog combo to minimize derailleur spring tension. While backpedaling slowly, watch the chain as it winds through the rear derailleur pulleys. If one link isn't bending like the others, it will be apparent. Loosen it by gripping the chain with your hands on either side of the tight link, then flexing it laterally. It helps to apply a drop of lube, too.

Brake squeal. Unless your shop road-tests each bike it sells, your brakes might shudder or squeal even if they were quiet on the test stand. Correcting this common malady involves angling each pad so the front ends contact the rim first. On some brakes, this toe-in adjustment is as simple as loosening the pads and retightening them (or their conical washers) in the proper position. With other brakes, it's accomplished by slightly bending the caliper arms.

Loose or creaking handlebar, stem, or saddle. If the handlebar slips in the stem, the stem rotates in the steerer tube, or the saddle moves in any direction, the part should be tightened immediately. In fact, every nut, bolt, and screw on the bike should be checked after the initial month of riding. Less apparent is the solution to creaking noises coming from any of these parts. They may be heard when pulling on the bar during climbs or sprints or when pedaling hard in the saddle. The place to start is with a light coating of grease where parts insert into the frame or into each other.

Gearing insufficiencies. If you ride in hilly terrain, you may desire lower gearing, particularly if your new bike is set up for racing and your legs and lungs are not. Conversely, a flatlander will find little use for wide-range touring gears and may want the greater efficiency of close-spaced ratios. A gearing swap can sometimes be negotiated before the bike leaves the showroom, but if you've ridden it for a few weeks and want to change cogs or chainrings, consider using the old parts as spares. Don't put up with a bike that isn't geared for your needs, even if it costs a bit extra to make it right.

Problematic pedals. If your bike came with clipless pedals and you're having difficulty with entry or release, the tension setting is too tight or there may be a compatibility problem between the cleats and your shoes. Let the shop know. The solution is usually as simple as adjusting the pedals' tension bolts.

Soft tires. Inner tubes are porous enough to slowly lose air. The higher the initial pressure, the faster this happens. Therefore, narrow road tires need air added more often than fat mountain bike tires. To prevent pinch flats and minimize rolling resistance, check tire pressure at least once each week. If one tire seems to lose air faster than the other, the valve may be faulty. Put it on your list of items for the 30-day checkup.

31
Postcrash Inspection

It rarely fails. The first words you hear as you help a rider up from a wreck are almost always, "How's my bike?" Forget the bruises and crash rash. Flesh heals, frames and components don't.

Hopefully, the unlucky rider can simply rotate the handlebar and brake levers to their proper positions and be on his or her way. But even when this is the case, it's best to examine the bike once back home. No one should risk a second accident due to a damaged part. Here's how to make a quick but thorough inspection.

Frame. In a front-end impact, the top and down tubes take much of the force. Inspect the area where these tubes join the head tube. Wrinkles or cracks in the paint indicate metal damage (see photo on page 116). The

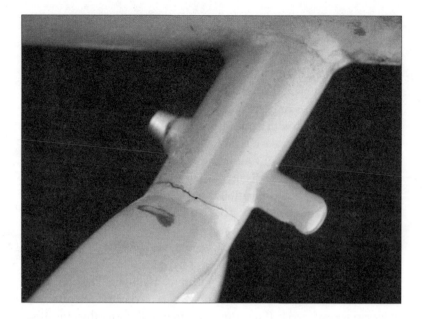

chainstays and seatstays can be bent, too. To check, sight down each one (though this will not be too revealing if the frame is built with curved stays). Then inspect the frame for dents. Sometimes the handlebar will swing around and strike the top tube hard enough to dimple it.

Small thumbprint-size dings and minor tube bends can be repaired by a framebuilder or mechanic who has an alignment table. More extreme damage may require replacing a tube or even discarding the frame.

Rigid fork. When you're looking from the side, a straight line through the center of the head tube should bisect the center of the fork's top section. Use a yardstick to help see this. If you find that the fork has been bent backward, the damage may be to the blades, steerer tube, or both. When the blades appear unharmed but the fork is out of alignment, remove it so the steerer can be inspected. Another check is to install an undamaged front wheel to see if the rim centers between the fork blades. If not, the blades were probably pushed to one side and must be straightened. Verify this by turning the wheel around to see if it remains off-center to the same side.

Have a qualified mechanic repair your fork using a jig and aligning lever. Sideways bends are easiest to fix. Fore/aft bends on high-quality forks can be remedied unless the blades are severely wrinkled or both the blades and steerer are bent. If in doubt, replace the fork.

Suspension fork. When a shock fork gets bent in a crash, it usually stops working correctly because the legs cannot telescope as before. Sometimes the bend occurs in the steerer tube, which is inside the head tube of the frame. This will cause binding in the steering. Both problems should be analyzed and repaired by qualified shop personnel. Often, parts of a shock fork can be replaced to repair crash damage. If not, you may have to replace the fork.

Wheels. Spin the wheels and look for lateral or vertical rim movement. Truing can correct some of this, but large wobbles, flat spots, or hops may necessitate replacing the rim and spokes. (It's not cost effective to replace these parts on an old or inexpensive hub. Instead, buy a new wheel.) Locate loose or broken spokes by wiggling each spoke of the wheel. In a violent crash, spokes can even pull out of the hub flange or cause it to crack. Replace spokes as necessary, tighten any loose ones, then true the wheel.

Feel for defects in the rim sidewall by holding your fingers against it as it spins. Bulges can sometimes be repaired by squeezing them with Channellock pliers, then sanding any roughness. Check for a bent axle by turning it with your fingers while looking directly into its end. If it has an out-of-round rotation, replace it. If the tire is flat because of cuts, tears, or other major damage to the tread or sidewall, install a new one.

Handlebar and stem. Look for scratches that indicate that these parts have been impacted and possibly damaged. To detect any abnormal bends, sight across the handlebar, then look from the front. Replace a bar rather than rebending it, which weakens it. Rotate the bar and stem to their correct positions after loosening the binder bolts with an allen wrench. Install new handlebar tape or grips, if necessary.

Brakes. A front caliper arm can bend in a crash when it swings around and strikes the down tube. Large pliers or an adjustable wrench can be used to straighten it. Go easy, or the alloy could snap. Replace brake-cable housing that has become kinked. Ditto for rubber hoods that have been torn. Inspect the left and right brake and shift levers for damage and orientation. If they've moved, loosen their clamps and rotate them into position. Levers with minor bends can be straightened or left alone. Replace any part that has more significant problems.

Derailleurs. When a bike falls over, it can land on the rear derailleur, bending it or the frame hanger inward toward the spokes. One sign of possible damage is a scuffed derailleur body. Also, look at your bike from behind. The derailleur cage should be parallel to the cogs. Misalignment should be corrected at a shop that has the tools to check and correct hanger position.

Pedals and crankarms. Carefully ride the bike to check for a bent pedal or crankarm. If there's damage, you'll feel it on each stroke. To pinpoint the problem, install a good pedal and ride some more. If your foot still feels weird, the crankarm is bent. It can probably be straightened by a mechanic. Bent pedals are iffy, but expensive ones are worth trying to save, possibly by installing a new axle.

Chainrings. Spin the crankset to see if the chainrings are true. Look from above, using the edge of the front derailleur cage as a guide. Chainring wobbles usually can be straightened with raps from a plastic mallet, bending with an adjustable wrench, or prying with a large screwdriver.

Saddle. The saddle usually gets scuffed in a crash, but this damage is cosmetic rather than structural. (It's why some mountain bike seats have bulletproof Kevlar protection on the rear corners.) However, a seat that looks or feels crooked after it's been realigned with the bike has bent or broken rails and must be replaced.

32
Pre-Event Checklist

There's an old maxim in bicycle racing that says, "In order to win, you have to finish." Fact is, this bit of wisdom applies to all cycling events— from low-key club rides to centuries—even if your "victory" is simply to post a good average speed or complete the distance. You may be in the best possible condition, but it won't matter if your bike breaks down.

The secret to making sure it doesn't is to conduct a thorough inspection two days before each important event. This allows time to test any adjustments you may need to make. Here's the checklist, arranged according to major areas of the bike. You'll need most of the "Basic" tools listed in chapter 1. For extra details about corrective procedures, turn to the appropriate chapter.

Drivetrain

Bottom bracket bearings. Shift to the small chainring. Use your finger to set the chain on the frame so it's out of the way. Spin the crankset while pressing an ear to the nose of the seat. The crankset should turn freely and sound smooth.

Wiggle the crankarms laterally to check for play. If there's looseness in a conventional cup-and-cone bottom bracket, remove it by using a lockring wrench and pin tool on the left-side adjustable cup. (This can usually be done without removing the crankarm.) Even if the bottom bracket feels okay, try tightening the lockring just to be sure it's snug.

On a cartridge crankset, remove the arms and check the axle's condition by wiggling and turning it with your fingers. If it spins smoothly with a light resistance, it's fine. The retainer rings may not be snug enough, so tighten the right side very firmly (counterclockwise because it has reverse threads), then tighten the left side(clockwise).

Crankarm bolts. Even if the bottom bracket checks out fine, remove the crankarm dustcaps (if applicable) and tighten the mounting bolts or nuts. Grease the caps' threads (if any) before reinstalling them.

Chainring bolts. Tighten these with a 5-mm allen wrench. You may need to hold the nuts on the back with a wide screwdriver or chainring bolt tool. Don't forget any bolts that attach from the back side.

Pedals. Tighten each one to the crankarm with a pedal wrench. Remember, the left pedal tightens counterclockwise. For clipless pedals, make sure the cleat-retention mechanisms are free of grimy buildup. For toeclips and straps, check for cracks where the clips attach and grooves that could cause straps to slip. Tighten the mounting hardware.

Chain. Backpedal with the chain in the small cog/chainring combo. If there are any stiff links, you'll notice them passing through the rear derailleur pulleys. To remedy a stiff link, grasp the chain on each side and flex laterally until the link loosens. Then lube it. (If there are more than two stiff links, replace the chain.)

Next, measure the chain with a 12-inch ruler. Start on the center of any pin and look at the 12-inch mark. If it's also on the center of a pin, the chain isn't worn. But if the second pin is $\frac{1}{8}$ inch or more past the foot mark, replace the chain.

After installing a new chain, you must take a short test ride to check for skipping. Carefully pedal forcefully in each gear. Skipping commonly occurs on smaller cogs because they wear the fastest. Replace individual cogs or the entire cluster as needed. If the current chain checks out fine, clean it (if necessary) and lube it.

Gear cables. Check for rusting or fraying at the levers, under the bottom bracket, at the derailleur anchor bolts, and everywhere a cable goes in or out of a guide or housing. Replace as necessary. Insert the nozzle tube into your can of spray lube and spritz each point where the cables contact anything.

Rear derailleur. Shift to make sure there's no hesitation when going to the largest or smallest cog. If shifting is sluggish or if the chain goes past these outermost cogs, adjust the limit screws. (They're sometimes marked L for the low-gear largest cog and H for high-gear smallest cog.)

To fine-tune an index system, use the adjustment barrel where the cable enters the derailleur. Turning the barrel counterclockwise takes up cable to quicken shifts to larger cogs. Turning it clockwise releases cable to improve shifts to smaller ones. Adjust it one-half turn at a time, then check performance in each direction.

Front derailleur. Shift forcefully, making sure the chain doesn't derail over the outside of the big ring or fall around the bottom bracket. Also check that the crankarm doesn't brush the cage when it's over the big ring. Make corrections by adjusting the limit screws.

Derailleur bolts. Gently tighten all bolts in the system. Don't forget the ones that attach the pulleys.

Rear Suspension

Pivots. Put a wrench on any and all pivot bolts and shock-attaching bolts to ensure that they're snug.

Preload. Check preload following the instructions in the owner's manual (see chapter 27 for tips) to make sure the shock is still set properly for your weight and that it will function optimally.

Wheels

Hub bearings. Remove both wheels. Turn and wiggle the axles with your fingers. Adjust the cones as necessary. Remember, proper adjustment leaves a hint of play to accommodate compression when the wheels are clamped into the frame. After the wheels are installed, recheck for play by trying to move them laterally. If you feel some, remove the wheel and tighten the cone adjustment.

Spokes. Wiggle each one. Tighten any loose ones with a spoke wrench until they're as taut as their same-side neighbors, then true the wheels.

Tires. Inflate to maximum recommended pressure (road) or the pressure that you've found is right for your weight and terrain (off-road). Tires should have ample tread thickness and no bulges or significant cuts. Also inspect the sidewalls for cracks or damage. Don't risk riding on suspect tires.

Brakes

Mounting bolts. Make sure the brakes are properly positioned, then snug the bolts that attach them to the frame.

Lubrication. Spray lube on the brake pivots and springs. Position a rag so you don't get any lube on the pads or tires.

Pads. If worn thinner than about 3 mm or to the point where any vertical grooves are gone, replace them. Be sure they strike the rim flush and cannot touch the tire or slip under toward the spokes. Also, orient them so their front ends touch the rims first when the brakes are applied. This prevents squealing. On some brakes, this toe-in is set with small washers, on others, the arms must be gently bent with leverage from an adjustable wrench.

Cables. Check for rust or fraying. Squeeze the levers and notice any sluggishness that means a problem inside the housing. If lubrication at the housing ends doesn't help, remove the cable. Clean and grease the enclosed sections or replace the housing.

Front End

Suspension fork. Check the preload setting, especially if the fork is air sprung. It's easy to add a little air if you have the correct pump and know what setting is correct for your weight (check the owner's manual). Also, snug all bolts on the fork, and check its action by compressing it several times and letting it rebound fully. If the travel seems minimal (most modern forks offer 2 to 4 inches), it's possible the fork needs an overhaul (usually a job for the shop).

Headset bearings. Turn the handlebar with the front wheel off the ground. If the fork turns roughly or incompletely, loosen the top nut and the adjustable cup underneath. Then tighten the nut and cup against each other. Check for looseness by rocking the bike back and forth while squeezing the front brake. Clunking means bearing play.

Another check is to lift the front end several inches and drop it, listening for a rattle. Tighten the bearing adjustment if necessary. Even if the headset passes these tests, make sure the nut and cone are tight against each other.

Handlebar and stem. Check stem tightness by turning the handlebar with the front wheel locked between your knees. You don't want the bar to pivot under moderate force, but it shouldn't be so tight that it can't move in a crash to lessen damage to the bike and your body. Press down on the ends of a drop bar to see if it rotates. Tighten the handlebar binder bolt, if necessary.

Levers. Check the tightness of all bar-mounted levers by trying to rotate them. Nothing should slip.

Saddle

Saddle and seatpost. Tighten the clamp at the top of the post. Try twisting the saddle/post. If it moves, snug the bolt where the seatpost enters the frame. Wrap a piece of electrical tape around the bottom of the post so you can tell if it starts slipping down. This also helps you re-install the seat at the correct height if you ever remove it.

Accessories

Bottle cages. Inspect them for cracks. Gently snug the mounting bolts. The same goes for any other bolt-on parts, such as racks or fenders.

Computer. Make sure the monitor, fork sensor, and wheel sensors are securely fastened. The wire should be taped or wrapped to eliminate slack so it can't snag something.

Repair kit. Examine your spare tube and patch kit. Make sure the glue hasn't dried and nothing has worn a hole in the tube. Include a piece of denim or old casing for covering the inside of a gash in a tire. Check the condition of your frame pump by using it to partially inflate a tire. Make sure your seatbag contains any other tools you need, wrapped snugly so they don't rattle. Stash $10 and some change for emergencies, plus your name, address, and the phone number of a person to contact.

33
Emergency Repair Kit

Perhaps the most satisfying use of the mechanical knowledge you gain from this book comes when you're able to repair your bike beside the road or trail. After all, it's when you're riding that malfunctions happen. Some won't let you ride safely or even ride at all until they're remedied.

To make a fix and get going again, you need a portable tool kit. It won't contain all of the items in your home shop, of course, because weight and bulk are important considerations on the bike. Here's how to assemble a suitably compact basic kit that you can take on every ride as well as a larger, more complete kit that you may carry on long-distance rides or tours, particularly in remote regions where no help is handy.

Mini-Kit

You should have a basic tool kit on any ride that takes you farther than you'd care to return on foot. In other words, consider this kit an essential bicycle component. It emphasizes efficiency, low weight, and minimal bulk. There are no extraneous items.

Frame pump. A full-size pump should wedge snugly under the top tube or in front of the seat tube. Most minipumps come with holders that fit under bottle-cage mounts or clamp to any frame tube. Be sure the pump head fits the valve type on your tubes.

Spare tube. Buy the correct size and valve. An ultralight model will save space and weight. Dust it with talcum powder, wrap it in a plastic bag, then put it back in its box for extra protection. Pack it in a way that prevents it from being chafed.

Patch kit. It should include a small tube of glue, four patches of various sizes, a piece of sandpaper, and a tire boot (make this out of a 1- by 1-inch piece of old tire casing or denim or canvas). Save a bit of space by using self-adhesive patches and omitting the glue if you like (just keep in mind that these patches are temporary). A boot is necessary in case of a large hole or cut in the tire. Tape the patch kit's lid to prevent it from accidentally opening.

Tire levers. It's nearly impossible to remove some high-pressure clinchers without levers. Save weight by choosing plastic ones instead of steel or aluminum. Although tire levers are normally sold in sets of three, you can get by with two.

Spoke wrench. Be sure it fits your spoke nipples. Some wrenches are more compact than others, so shop around.

Chain rivet extractor. This is essential for mountain biking, where snapped chains are not uncommon. If your bike has a Shimano Hyperglide chain, you also need to carry several replacement pins.

All-in-one tool. Several companies make ingenious devices that include virtually every essential small tool in one compact unit. Among the array should be allen wrenches, wrench fittings, and screwdrivers. Some models even include the above-mentioned tire levers, spoke wrench, and chain tool.

Small jackknife. You need a sharp blade, and a model that also includes an awl, file, scissors, and other tools can come in very handy. Don't overdo it. Some bicycle mini-tools include these items, too.

Odds and ends. Carry a presta-to-Schrader valve adapter (in case your pump breaks), a couple of spare chainring bolts, change for the telephone, food money, a spare house key, and an identification card. The change is for calling help when all else fails. The food money gives you the freedom to extend a ride without bonking. Remember to restock the stuff after you dip in to it.

Seatbag. To store everything, buy an under-saddle bag that's only slightly larger than you need. Even better, get one that's expandable to hold the odd extra item.

Maxi-Kit

On all-day or multiday excursions, the following items should be added to your basic kit. Because there isn't a pro bike shop around every corner, this stuff is intended to bail you out of almost any mechanical difficulty that can occur. (Of course, don't bother carrying a tool that you don't know how to use—unless you intend to pack this book, too.) You can assemble all of the tools piecemeal or buy one of the well-stocked portable kits that several companies make. Prices range upward from about $60, and the kits include a compartmentalized carrying case.

Folding tire and extra tube. Those of you who've asked for a 700C tire or presta-valve tube at the hardware store in Podunk, USA, will appreciate the need to carry these spares on an extended ride. Folding tires with Kevlar beads are available in virtually all sizes, including mountain bike dimensions.

Spare spokes. Carry several of each size that your wheels require. Keep them inside the frame pump or, if that's not possible, taped atop the left chainstay.

Spare cables. Properly maintained cables shouldn't break, but if they do, nothing will work in their place. Carry a brake cable and a rear derailleur cable (with the unneeded head removed if you buy the universal type). If a cable breaks, install the replacement and coil the excess until you can trim it.

Cassette remover. Cassette removal is necessary for spoke replacement on the right side of the hub. You need a chain whip, too, so a handy tool is the Park HCW-14, which combines a whip with a headset wrench. Make sure another of the tools you pack will fit and turn the cassette remover.

Crankarm bolt wrench (sometimes included in the all-in-one tool). A loose crankarm is a real nuisance. Crankarm bolts may loosen slightly, but they won't be able to work their way out if dustcaps are installed. So if your bike has dustcaps, make sure you use them.

Adjustable cup tools. Park makes lightweight universal pin tools and lockring tools. These are indispensable for adjusting a conventional bottom bracket that has loosened. Otherwise, you'll grind the bearings into pulp as you pedal toward the closest bike shop. If your bike has a cartridge bottom bracket and you've checked its tightness during routine service, you shouldn't need to worry about its coming loose. However, a retainer ring tool is a small item to pack for peace of mind.

Adjustable wrench. The 6-inch size is handy for removing pedals and straightening chainrings.

Channellock pliers. A small pair will do what the other tools won't.

Lubricants. Pack a small tube of grease and a small bottle of chain lube in zip-shut plastic bags.

Hand cleaner. Store a tube of this and some paper towels in zip-shut plastic bags.

Bike trunk. To carry all of these items, you need something in addition to your seatbag. If you're touring with panniers, there will be ample room. If not, a good solution is a rectangular bag or trunk that sits atop a rear rack. It should have several zippered pockets and an expandable center cavity that has room for other items, too. Another type supports the bag on a platform that attaches to the seatpost. No rack is needed. If using panniers, pack the tools at the bottom. Hopefully, you won't need to get at them often, and this location helps bike handling by lowering the center of gravity.

Anatomy of a Bike

saddle rails
*(saddle can be slid forward
or backward along these)*

saddle

seatpost
*(holds saddle and
determines its tilt)*

seatpost quick-release
*(allows saddle to be raised
or lowered without tools)*

seat tube
(length determines frame size)

rear brake
(cantilever also available)

seatstay

freewheel or cassette
*(collection of five to nine cogs
of varied number of teeth)*

chainstay

chain

rear dropout
*(slots in which rear
hub axle fits)*

cable housing
(routes and protects wire cable)

derailleur adjustment barrel
*(allows fine-tuning of cable
length; similar mechanism
may be found on brakes)*

rear derailleur
*(moves chain from cog to cog;
controlled by right shift lever)*

derailleur pulleys
(direct chain through rear derailleur)

cable stop
*(anchors the housing for
the cable to pull against)*

front derailleur
*(moves chain from chainring
to chainring; controlled by
left shift lever)*

triple chainring
*(provides wide-range
gearing for climbing and
high-speed riding)*

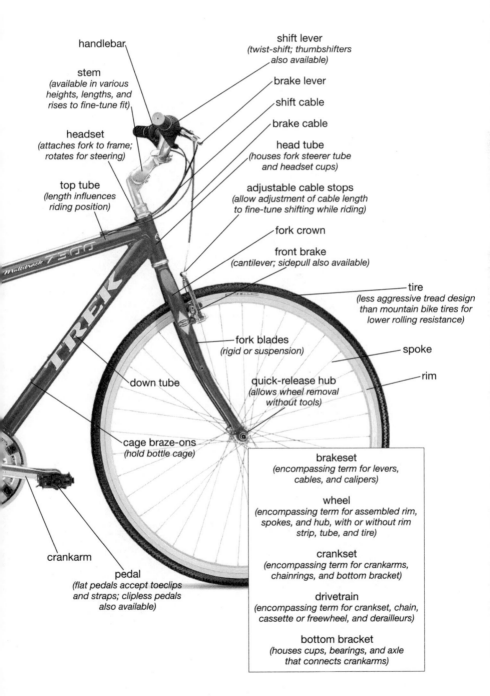

handlebar

stem
*(available in various
heights, lengths, and
rises to fine-tune fit)*

headset
*(attaches fork to frame;
rotates for steering)*

top tube
*(length influences
riding position)*

shift lever
*(twist-shift; thumbshifters
also available)*

brake lever

shift cable

brake cable

head tube
*(houses fork steerer tube
and headset cups)*

adjustable cable stops
*(allow adjustment of cable length
to fine-tune shifting while riding)*

fork crown

front brake
(cantilever; sidepull also available)

tire
*(less aggressive tread design
than mountain bike tires for
lower rolling resistance)*

fork blades
(rigid or suspension)

spoke

rim

quick-release hub
*(allows wheel removal
without tools)*

down tube

cage braze-ons
(hold bottle cage)

crankarm

pedal
*(flat pedals accept toeclips
and straps; clipless pedals
also available)*

brakeset
*(encompassing term for levers,
cables, and calipers)*

wheel
*(encompassing term for assembled rim,
spokes, and hub, with or without rim
strip, tube, and tire)*

crankset
*(encompassing term for crankarms,
chainrings, and bottom bracket)*

drivetrain
*(encompassing term for crankset, chain,
cassette or freewheel, and derailleurs)*

bottom bracket
*(houses cups, bearings, and axle
that connects crankarms)*

Index

Underscored page references indicate boxed text.
Boldface references indicate photographs.